PRAISE FOR
THE MARRIAGE HABIT

"With simple, actionable habits and down-to-earth guidance, Meygan and Casey show exactly how to stay connected, communicate better, and nurture a marriage that truly supports the whole family."

—Amy McCready, founder of Positive Parenting Solutions and author of *The Me, Me, Me Epidemic*

"Casey and Meygan are true warriors for marriage—steadfastly devoted to helping couples stay connected and thrive. If you're looking for tools to deepen your connection and strengthen your bond, *The Marriage Habit* will truly transform your relationship."

—Laurie Watson, PhD, sex therapist and co-host of the *Brave Love* podcast

"Few marriage books make it this easy to apply powerful truths. If you want to get out of the trap of endless blaming, pointing fingers, and feeling hopelessly frustrated in your marriage, *The Marriage Habit* turns timeless wisdom into daily action."
—Quentin Hafner, LMFT, founder of Black Belt Husband

"I don't want advice from a married couple who has never had any conflict. Casey and Meygan's openness and vulnerability about their marriage, on the brink of divorce, is what drew me to their books and courses. They've been through the hardest times and come back from it, marriage still intact—and *that's* who I want to learn from."
—Erin Washington, host of *thERINpy with Erin Washington*

"We've journeyed through ups and downs in three decades of marriage, and we know it's possible to come out even stronger. *The Marriage Habit* offers couples real hope and practical habits to do just that"
—Bret Johnson, husband, dad, and entrepreneur

"If you're looking for a couple who is both wildly enthusiastic and super strategic about helping marriages in the real world, you won't find a better couple than Meygan and Casey. Couples are drawn to them because they are so real, and that same authenticity comes through on every page. *The Marriage Habit* is practical, approachable, and actually doable. It doesn't just tell you what to do, it gives you the tools to do it. This book sparks meaningful conversations without being heavy, and I can't wait for couples to start living out *The Marriage Habit*."
—Ted Lowe, founder of For Us Marriage

"*The Marriage Habit* offers couples practical, actionable steps to transform their relationship from ordinary to extraordinary. Casey and Meygan Caston understand that thriving marriages don't happen by accident—they're built through intentional daily practices. If you want to be more than just roommates with your spouse, this is the book for you. These ten simple practices will help you create deeper connection, stronger communication, and a more fulfilling partnership. Whether you're newly married or decades in, this book provides the tools you need to build the marriage you've always wanted."

—Debbie and Jim Hogan, co-founders of Standing Stone Ministry and authors of *Shepherding Shepherds*

ALSO BY
CASEY and MEYGAN CASTON

365 Connecting Questions for Couples
(Revised & Updated)

THE
MARRIAGE
HABIT

THE MARRIAGE HABIT

10 Simple Practices
to Build a More Intentional,
Thriving Relationship

Casey and Meygan Caston

CONVERGENT
New York

Convergent
An imprint of Random House
A division of Penguin Random House LLC
1745 Broadway, New York, NY 10019
convergentbooks.com
penguinrandomhouse.com

Hardcover ISBN 978-0-593-73640-1
Ebook ISBN 978-0-593-73641-8

Printed in the United States of America

1st Printing

First Edition

BOOK TEAM: Production editor: Abby Duval • Managing editor: Allison Fox • Production manager: Maggie Hart • Copy editor: Whitney Bak Proofreaders: Rachael Clements, Kathy Mosier, Robin Slutzky, and Anya Getschel

Title-page circle pattern: kasheev/Adobe Stock

Book design by Alexis Flynn

The authorized representative in the EU for product safety and compliance is Penguin Random House Ireland, Morrison Chambers, 32 Nassau Street, Dublin D02 YH68, Ireland.
https://eu-contact.penguin.ie

For Cesar and Patty—
our lifelong friends who are now family.
Thank you for being with us through
the highest of highs and lowest of lows.
We love you both.

CONTENTS

AUTHORS' NOTE

At the end of each chapter, you'll find a section called "Connecting Questions." At Marriage365, questions are the foundation of everything we do. The ones in this book are intended to guide you as you learn about and implement each habit with your spouse, or a safe friend if your spouse isn't on board yet. (You can also use the questions as journal prompts.) If you love these questions and want more, check out our first book, *365 Connecting Questions for Couples*. The road to healing our marriage began with Meygan asking Casey a single open-ended question. We wish the same for you.

This book is written by both of us, so you'll occasionally encounter when we swap between using the pronoun *we* and, when one of us is telling a story about the other, *he* or *she*. That's intentional. We're always speaking as a couple.

You'll also see mention throughout the book of supplementary materials you can download to help you work through each habit. You can find those at Marriage365Books.com/resources.

—Casey and Meygan

If You Want to Make a Better Marriage . . .

Do you remember how much fun dating was? We sure do. We met in college, when Meygan was eighteen and Casey was twenty-two. Casey was on the freshmen welcoming committee, and Meygan was a doe-eyed freshman. It was love at first sight. (Or as close as it gets, anyway.) From day one, we were *into* each other. Sparks flew, the chemistry was real, we had googly eyes and hearts aflutter. We simply couldn't get enough of each other. Maybe you know the feeling.

Not long after, Meygan was asleep in her second-story dorm when she heard a faint sound. *Dink, dink.* It was ten o'clock (Meygan: *Not my usual bedtime, but I had a big test the next day and was trying to be responsible*), and something was hitting her window. She climbed out of bed wearily and went to the glass.

Casey was throwing pebbles from the ground, motioning for her to open the window. "Hey! Come down here, I have a surprise." (Casey: *I had a test the next day too, but I cared less about getting good grades.*) Meygan hesitated. She'd been studying all day. Spontaneity was not in her nature. It still isn't. If you were to think of a word that *least* describes Meygan, it might be *spontaneous*. But Casey was and is incredibly spontaneous, down to his core. Though it was so "*not* Meygan" to jump out of bed and run down for a late-night surprise, something in her sparked. The opportunity was enticing exactly because it was so out of her element. She grabbed a sweatshirt and ran downstairs. There stood Casey with his big blue eyes and signature grin.

We went down to the beach, where we walked and talked until two o'clock. It was the kind of "date" where you lose track of time and your surroundings because you're so absorbed in the other person. In fact, it was so foggy we could barely see past our noses and lost our shoes in the sand. Normally Meygan would have been irritated about this, but that night, uncharacteristically, she couldn't have cared less. When she finally crawled back into bed in the early hours of the morning, she was still buzzing with excitement. *Wow, I think I love this guy.* Casey skipped home barefoot, thinking the exact same thing about her.

Over the next few months, there were many more Casey-instigated surprises and spontaneous dates. Our days together were fun and wildly different from anything Meygan would have chosen on her own. Likewise, Casey appreciated that Meygan kept so much of our slowly, ever-combining lives organized. She's a planner, through and through. She always knew where we needed to be and when and helped him think through big decisions. Casey had a revolving door of stepfathers throughout his childhood, and Meygan's stability became a lifeline. He loved that about her. We made each other better and helped pick up slack where the other person was weak. Then, less than a year later, like most people who fall in love, we figured, "Hey, why don't we do this forever?" And so we made a commitment and sealed it with "I do."

However, that appreciation for each other's differences didn't last forever. (Stop us if you've heard this before.) After a few years of marriage, Casey's spontaneity no longer seemed cute. When he suggested a last-minute trip to the mountains one day while Meygan was knee-deep in work emails, she wasn't charmed like she'd been that night with the pebbles—she was irritated.

"I can't just drop everything and go!" she snapped. "We have responsibilities and a busy schedule!"

That trait she'd loved so much about Casey was now a nuisance, a liability. And Casey felt shut down. . . . again. "You never want to do anything fun anymore," he replied. While Meygan's organization and planning skills kept our life running smoothly, Casey felt like there was no room to let go and do something out of the ordinary, something to keep life interesting. Meygan didn't want interesting and spontaneous. She wanted predictable and safe. Things weren't at all like they used to be, in more ways than just this one.

We thought our wedding day would kick off an amazing season of our lives. It actually began the slow decline of our relationship. Some rock bottoms are a quick *thunk*, a huge event that plummets you right to the basement of life. Like getting pulled over for DUI or the moment you get caught cheating. Ours was more like *thuuuuuuuuuuuuuuunk*. Within just a few years of meeting each other, we'd built up more than $250,000 of debt and been through dozens of jobs. We walked through eighteen months of infertility and parenting a child with disabilities (plus a husband with severe ADHD). We discovered that we were more different than alike, and we didn't know how to turn that into a strength. It was a long, difficult season filled with months of fighting and hurting each other and feeling utterly alone. Death by a thousand cuts, as they say.

We didn't do any of this on purpose. Despite being desperately in love (and we were), we checked just about every box on the marriage checklist of doom. For starters, there are twelve marriages between our two sets of parents, and multiple affairs in there too. Casey describes his childhood home as a constant revolving door of fathers. His mother had six husbands, and he'd endured ten different iterations of a homelife before junior high. Say it with us: yikes. Neither of us had a single example in our lives of what a healthy, long-term relationship looked like. And the ways we *were* alike seemed to just complicate things further. We're both strong and stubborn, and we each like to lead. We had no idea how to communicate, apologize, take feedback, offer help, or have sex.

In short: We had no idea how to love each other. Was this really what marriage was supposed to be like? We didn't want to give up, but we couldn't keep going like this either.

At our lowest point, Meygan went to see a counselor, even though we couldn't afford it and Casey wouldn't go with her. This was what finally started our journey back to each other. (We'll get into that more throughout the book.) We read books, took courses, studied data, and sought mentorship and healing. After eight years of hard work, we'd finally come to a place where we felt deeply satisfied with our marriage and knowledgeable about how to love each other and problem-solve together. Our marriage evolved into the source of strength, love, and security we'd always hoped it would be. Along the way, almost accidentally, we started helping other couples do the same.

Turns out, we hadn't been as unique in our struggle as we thought. When we shared our insights in church groups and on social media, we began getting feedback on how useful and relatable our content was. Now, each day, we get two hundred to three hundred messages from spouses looking for advice and, mostly, hope. What a strange and humbling place to be in. Especially since, for years, we felt more like experts on how to dismantle a marriage than experts on how to put one back together.

So we started Marriage365, a platform that helps partners heal and strengthen their relationships. For more than a decade now we've helped millions of people work on their partnerships. We've helped dating couples decide whether they should get married. We've walked struggling couples back from the brink of divorce. We've counseled empty nesters in their new chapter of life without kids. We've led people in affair recovery. Through all this, we've become nationally recognized marriage coaches.

We're not gurus or academics who speak in fancy words and concepts; we're your average neighborhood couple who walked through fire, got some scars, learned a lot, and want to share that knowledge to help others. It is one of the greatest honors of our lives to motivate couples to be more intentional in their marriages and help individuals become the healthiest versions of themselves.

We've learned that marriage advice needs to be practical and tactical, not just inspirational. You can't theorize your way out of resentment. You can't throw a platitude at an angry spouse and expect that to improve things. You can't even sit with a counselor and talk your way into a connected and nurturing marriage. Deep down, most of us know what we need to do: be kind, love each other, communicate, listen intently, and be good partners. But what most people don't know is *how* to do it. How much knowledge have we collected over the years from books and authorities that turned out to be useless because we still have no idea how to implement it?

We love therapy. We fully endorse it as a way to process hurt, understand yourself better, and grapple with the impact of mental health issues. But what we've heard over and over again from couples who have been in and out of therapy for years is this: They still don't know what to actually *do* to improve their relationship. And as much as therapy has helped us and others along the way, here's a truth we discovered as we journeyed back to each other and coached others to do the same: *Most couples don't need more therapy; they just need better tools.*

During those years when we were fumbling and trying to fix our relationship, we discovered something that changed our view of marriage. It wasn't big trips, occasional grand gestures, or one obligatory date night per month that brought us back together and kept our love strong. It was the regular, small, daily habits that we'd developed. We synced our calendars, said "thank you," made Love Lists, went on walks, used a code word when things got tense, spontaneously apologized, put our phones away at dinner, and complimented each other every day. You don't need grand gestures or deep counseling sessions every week to have a great marriage—you need repeatable moments of connection, kindness, and repair.

You've come to the right book if any of these resonate:

- *You feel like roommates instead of partners.* We've felt this one deeply. It's so easy to fall into the routines of everyday life and forget to keep intentionally loving each other. Your conversations become transactional and surface level, only about chores, kids, or schedules. Your parallel lives look like train tracks moving in the same direction but never intersecting.

- *You argue over the smallest things.* This is a common one. Often, it's not our unexamined childhood trauma that sets us off but the fact that our spouse forgot (again) to take out the freaking trash. Don't get us wrong, your childhood trauma might be getting in the way of your relationship. But people underestimate the power of solving the simpler problems to restore connection.

- *You don't feel like a team anymore.* One of our favorite analogies about marriage is that it's like being on a team. You'll hear it a lot throughout this book. It's painful to feel like you've lost a teammate, like your partner isn't in your corner anymore. You're not opponents; you're not trying to win against each other. You're working with each other toward the same goals—connection, peace, growth, and trust.

- *You miss the spark you once had.* Whether it's physical, emotional, or both, one of the most common complaints we hear from couples is that they feel like the spark is gone. It's true—over time, your spouse might not be as mysterious to you as they once were, but that doesn't have to mean your level of intimacy declines. The spark isn't only about pheromones and banter; it's also a connection that is built and available to you at any point in your marriage.

- *You believe marriage can and should be a tremendous source of joy in your life.* You're right! Whether you're already living this out or it's not even close to your reality, your belief is the point. Marriage can and should be one of the best, most fun, most uplifting experiences of your life. If you still believe in that promise, you're in the right place.

Maybe you don't identify strongly with any of these points. Maybe your marriage is already a source of love and security, and you just want to keep strengthening it over time. That's great too! All of that brings us to this book.

In these pages, we're going to detail the ten marriage habits that the healthiest couples we've worked with have in common. These are the tools that saved our marriage, the set of habits that keep us connected and growing together. It's a set of practices you can learn and start implementing today to build or rebuild the relationship you've always wanted. They're teachable, accessible, and free ways to create the lifelong marriage of your dreams. The couples who do these things are the ones we've seen go the distance. They experience true connection and joy in their relationship. They're happy, secure, respectful, united, and stronger together than they are apart. The wisdom in these pages is easy enough to implement right now, without the academic, impractical, over-your-head jargon.

If you're going through this book by yourself and your spouse isn't on board yet, that's okay. You're in good company. In fact, it's rare for both people to be on board in exactly the same way at exactly the same time with exactly the same amount of effort. Of the many thousands of people who use our Marriage365 app, most are using it on their own. More than 60 percent of our members join without their partner's participation. Which is why all of our tools can be done on your own, regardless of your spouse's involvement level.

Hear this loud and clear: You are not stuck simply because you can't change your partner. We've watched thousands of marriages experience a turnaround, and almost always, someone is more engaged than the other at the start. So here's the best piece of marriage advice we have: If you want to make a better marriage, it starts with making a better you. If you are looking for a book that will change your spouse, reveal how wrong they are, and prove just how right you are . . . well, friends, keep on looking. This is about you, the only person you can control. You don't have to wait for your spouse to join. Start now, with yourself.

Over the lifetime of a marriage, it does take two people to make it last, and there are a few situations we want to address. If you are in an abusive relationship—emotionally, physically, sexually, or financially—these principles and habits may not apply. Your safety comes first, and we encourage you to seek professional help and support right away.

Remember, you already know how to do this. You did it before. You wooed your spouse and forged a connection deep enough for you to decide to spend your life together. You don't need lots of money or time. You just need the commitment and courage to try. Believe us; if we can do it, you can too.

PART I

What No One Told You
About Marriage

"WHY DOES THIS FEEL SO HARD?"

●━━━━━━━━━━━━━━━━━━━━━━━●

One Saturday early in our marriage, we were at Target running errands—a typical weekend activity. We'd gone there to grab a few essentials like toilet paper and dish soap, but of course Meygan was hoping for a little time to peruse. It was a Saturday morning, after all. We had the day off and didn't have kids yet, so the scenario was primed for browsing through books or bath towels or tchotchkes. That dream died as soon as we walked inside. The store was packed. Kids were running through the aisles, and carts with squeaky wheels swerved all over the place. It was absolute pandemonium. Our blood pressures rose as we navigated the madhouse. All we wanted was to get what we'd come for and leave quickly, without any drama.

In fairness, we were already on edge that morning. It was one of those days where you look at each other and wonder, *Are you just here to ruin my day?* Every little comment was biting, and the tension was thick. Then the throngs of people bumping us took it to the next level. Meygan, being a problem solver, suggested a solution. "Hey, I'll grab the car, and you check out, and I'll meet you outside." It was a perfect plan, except for the part where Casey didn't hear her. He had a classic ADHD moment and was immersed in his decision about which alarm clock he should pick. When he came out of his trance, Meygan was nowhere to be found. He looked around, panicked. *Where in the world did she go? Did she hate it so much in here that she just bailed without saying anything?*

After racing up and down aisles, Casey was so nervous—heart pounding—that he abandoned the cart and ran outside to look for Meygan. That's when he saw her pulling up the car to the entrance, smiling. He stormed over, slammed his hand on the window, and screamed, "You LEFT me!" He literally yelled it. A lady nearby gasped in horror and pulled her son closer. (When you're scaring casual Target-goers, you know you've crossed the line.)

Meygan stared at him, shocked and confused. She thought she was being wife of the year, pulling up the car to rescue him from the suburban chaos. Casey huffed inside the car and sat in silence, glaring out the window. Meygan tried to explain that she'd told him what she was going to do, but he didn't want to hear it. He was fuming.

We'd already been having a rough morning. Now the rest of the day would be ruined. We both knew we'd stew on that incident for hours, incapable of having a healthy conversation about it. There might be a snide remark here or there. If we really worked ourselves up, maybe we'd have a screaming match at dinner, and that would be that.

As we drove the car home—Casey staring out the passenger-side window and Meygan in the driver's seat, confused and on the verge of tears—we both had the same thought: *I didn't expect marriage to be like this.* Dating had felt largely fun and carefree, even easy. Whatever this was, it wasn't that. What changed?

A TALE AS OLD AS TIME

How many times have you heard this in books, conversations, and society at large: *Marriage is hard.* Countless times, right? But why does this cliché ring true for so many couples? And why would so many people sign up for an experience that's mainly known for being hard? I mean, married people love each other, right? Isn't love supposed to be enough? What's the point of being married if it makes us feel miserable and if there's a good chance we'll end up divorced anyway?

These are all good questions. As far as institutions go, marriage is one of the oldest. It's been around for just about as long as we've had recorded history—more than five thousand years—and it's taken many different forms since then. Here's a lightning-round version of that history. Back in ancient Greece, marriage was more like a business transaction than a love story. For centuries, its purpose remained largely the same. People married to climb political and social ladders. Women were essentially property, and the whole point was to secure land, heirs, and political alliances. Love had nothing to do with it. Fast-forward a few thousand years, and marriage became a way to manage households, raise children, and keep society running smoothly with gender-divided roles. The romance piece was still very optional.

It wasn't until a few hundred years ago that love entered the picture. As society advanced and more rights and options became available (mostly to women), people started marrying for companionship, affection, and attraction. Obviously, on the whole, this was great. You could choose who you married and make sure you actually liked the person! Women had more of a say in their future! But with that shift came a whole new set of expectations. Now, not only were we supposed to manage finances, raise kids, and keep the house clean, but we were also supposed to be madly in love and sexually compatible the entire time.

As the purpose of marriage shifted, rom-coms and romance

novels further advanced the notion that a relationship should look and feel a certain way all the time (a certain hearts-and-chocolates, bubble-baths-filled kind of way). And the rest of modern life hasn't made marriage any easier. Couples used to live with entire communities around them to help. When you had a baby, your family and neighbors would swoop in, cooking meals, holding the baby, and giving you a chance to sleep. Now, with the shift toward individualistic nuclear families, most of us are out here doing it alone, thinking we're failing because we can't do it all by ourselves. It puts enormous pressure on marriages to be everything: companionship, emotional support, co-parenting, financial partnership, and sometimes even the only opportunity for adult conversation we have all week.

In short: Don't be hard on yourself. These days, so much about society sets us up to fail when it comes to our relationships. It's no wonder we're struggling.

THE MYTHS

In our work with thousands of couples, we've found that these social advancements and messages from popular culture—many of them positive—have contributed to a set of myths people believe about their marriages. The first thing we do in coaching is dismantle these lies. Because yes, marriage can be hard, but it's made exponentially harder if you have one of these three falsehoods rolling around in your brain.

Myth 1: "If it were true love, it wouldn't be this hard."

We fell for this one hook, line, and sinker. It is a real heartbreaker. We believed that if our love was *real*, it would be easy. That any struggles or challenges must mean there was something wrong with our relationship. When things got tough, we didn't ask ourselves, *How can we work through this?* Instead, we asked, *Is this even real love?*

[Quick caveat here: When we say "hard," we are *not* talking about the four A's—abuse, affairs, addiction, and abandonment. Those are severe physical and mental health issues that are beyond the scope of this book. We are not talking about *that* kind of hard. If you've experienced any of these, we recommend you get somewhere safe and seek professional help.]

This is the kind of thinking that leads you to question everything after your first big fight, which in our case was over the proper way to load the dishwasher. We wish we were kidding. In the early years of our marriage, we fought about the dishwasher like it was the key to our relationship's survival. There was yelling, there were tears, and once, for a moment, we were pretty sure this was *it*. This was the end of our love story, all because Casey didn't align the spoons in the cutlery tray the "right way."

How many times have you wondered if you were truly in love simply because your relationship didn't feel easy? The reality is, love is not a feeling. Or rather, it's not *just* a feeling. Feelings are fickle—they come and go depending on how much sleep you've had or whether your spouse accidentally (or "accidentally") ate the last piece of cake. Real love is a choice. It's a habit. It's deciding every day, even when you're angry or tired or feeling unappreciated, to be kind, to communicate, and to keep showing up.

Research backs this up. Psychologist Dr. Gary Lewandowski, Jr., has found that successful marriages aren't the ones where the couple never fights (spoiler: They don't exist). Successful marriages are the ones where both people are committed to working through the tough stuff together. It turns out that fighting is normal; how you fight and how you repair afterward make all the difference. We had to learn that the hard way, after many fights and many failed attempts at repair.

Of course, you can still be very much in love and walk through seriously hard times in your marriage. It doesn't mean you've married the wrong person or that your relationship is doomed when the going gets tough. Which leads us to myth number two . . .

Myth 2: "Marriage should make me happy."

Here's the truth: It's not your spouse's job to make you happy. It's *your* job to make you happy. Marriage isn't about finding someone who completes you (thanks for nothing, Jerry Maguire). It's about finding someone who will partner with you while you work on becoming a complete person yourself. That's why our slogan at Marriage365 is a riff on that best piece of advice we mentioned earlier: If you want to make a better marriage, make a better you.

This was a hard pill for the two of us to swallow. We both had moments when we looked at each other and thought, *You're not making me happy anymore. What's the point?* But happiness is fleeting. It comes and goes, and if you put all the pressure on your spouse to make you feel validated and fulfilled, you're going to end up disappointed. Instead, each of us started focusing on how we could make ourselves happier—working on our own mental health, finding hobbies we enjoyed, and being responsible for our own joy. And guess what? It made our marriage stronger.

Research shows that people in happy marriages aren't necessarily happier because of their marriage. They're happier because they take care of themselves, they have realistic expectations, and they don't rely on their partners to fulfill every need. When we both started taking responsibility for our own happiness, we were able to show up for each other in a way that made our relationship better. Don't get us wrong, your marriage should greatly contribute to your happiness. But it is not the sole responsibility of your partner or your relationship to make you happy. That's not *why* you get married.

There's an old rom-com with Ashton Kutcher and Brittany Murphy called *Just Married.* It's about a young couple (Tom and Sarah) who start off madly in love. They get married very quickly and then absolutely nothing goes according to plan. Tom accidentally shuts down an entire European village's electricity, their rental car crashes in a snowbank in the French Alps, and they run into Sarah's snobby ex-boyfriend who happens to be staying in the same hotel. After a honeymoon from hell, they decide to go their separate ways, only to change their minds and realize they really do love each other and want to fight for the marriage. At the end of that silly but fun movie is a very poignant scene with Tom's dad. He says to Tom, "You never see the hard days in a photo album, but those are the ones that get you from one happy snapshot to the next."

You will have plenty of happy days. But you will also have unhappy days in between. That's no one's fault. It's just how life works. Take the pressure off your spouse to make all your days happy.

MEYGAN'S INSIGHT

One of the biggest traps women fall into is the comparison game—especially with what we see on social media and TV. You watch highlight reels of men planning extravagant dates or saying all the right things, and suddenly you're looking at your husband, thinking, *Why can't he be more like that?* That kind of constant comparison breeds disappointment and resentment. Instead of measuring your marriage against filtered half-truths, focus on what's real and meaningful in your relationship.

Myth 3: "I should know how to do this."

This final myth might be the most insidious of all, because it's the one that keeps people from asking for help. It is the widespread idea that we should just *know* how to be married. I mean, most people get married, right? How hard could it be? But if you've been married for any length of time, you probably already know it's not that simple.

The truth is, most of us walk into marriage with zero training.

We learn algebra in school—which, by the way, neither of us has used since—but we don't learn how to communicate effectively, how to manage conflict, or how to compromise without feeling like we're losing. We bring our family dynamics, our baggage, and our unrealistic expectations into this new relationship and then wonder why it feels impossible.

Here's what we've learned: No one knows what they're doing. And that's okay. Marriage is a skill. And like any skill, it takes practice, patience, and a willingness to learn. It's perfectly normal if you feel like you don't know how to be married, even if you're decades in. It doesn't mean that you're bad at it or that you can't still have the marriage of your dreams.

CASEY'S COACHING CORNER

I encounter this all the time when coaching men, and I wish wives understood it more about their husbands. Many men grew up with emotionally absent fathers and without role models. This leaves them clueless and frustrated. They want great marriages, but they don't know how to achieve them. Often the result is that they bury themselves in work because it's an area of their lives where they feel they are winning.

In our work with couples, we've seen these myths push countless marriages to their breaking points. Spouses spend so much time thinking they're failing because their relationship isn't living up to some unrealistic standard—that love should be easy, that they should always make each other happy, and that they should just know how to do this. Marriage is many things (we'd argue it's the best thing). It's frustrating and wonderful and sometimes just plain boring. A happy marriage is not about being perfect; it's about being willing to grow, to learn, and to choose each other, even on the hard days.

In the chapters that follow, we're going to teach you many practical ways to strengthen, heal, and improve your marriage. Things are about to get good. Don't carry the baggage of these falsehoods that make you feel like you're failing any longer. You're not. You just need some guidance and a little practice.

When the two of us began letting go of these myths, we started to find our rhythm. We learned how to communicate better, how to handle conflict, and how to repair after the inevitable arguments. We learned that it's okay to ask for help, to admit we don't know everything, and to laugh at ourselves when we mess up—because we do, A LOT.

No, our marriage didn't turn out to be the fairy tale we once thought it might be when we were dating. It's *better*. Because it's *real*. At the end of the day, that's why people keep engaging in this thousands-year-old institution—because of all the things marriage can be. At its best, marriage means regular sleepovers with your best friend. It means always having someone in your corner. It makes the lows of life not nearly as low and the highs even higher because you're walking through them with someone you love deeply. A healthy, long-lasting marriage means security, fun, partnership, great sex, and a witness to your life. It's the deepest, most intimate kind of connection. That's why people keep getting married, despite the odds and obstacles today.

That's what we want for each of you. And here's another surprising truth: Marriage doesn't actually have to be that hard. In fact, it probably shouldn't be. Your marriage can be a source of joy in your life that makes each of you stronger and better.

CONNECTING QUESTIONS

1. What were some of the biggest assumptions you had about marriage before we got married?

2. How do you think personal happiness and marital happiness are connected?

3. How have your views about marriage and love been influenced by social media, your upbringing, or what you watch on TV?

4. Why do you think challenges are an inevitable part of a lasting relationship?

5. How do we typically respond to challenges in our marriage? Do we work as a team or pull apart?

6. What are some ways we can support each other when marriage feels difficult?

THE ONLY TWO THINGS YOU NEED

It was a quiet evening in our cramped two-bedroom apartment many years ago. We had both just finished work. Meygan got home first and was in the thick of cooking dinner on the stove with a crying baby at her feet. We found ourselves standing in the tiny kitchen space in the middle of what should have been a normal evening conversation: "How was your day? Did you call the plumber? Did you hear about so-and-so? My boss did something annoying again." But Casey was deeply engaged in his phone, still trying to wrap up a lingering work issue, and Meygan was desperate for help. With the baby. With dinner. With anything. Because we were very much Casey and Meygan 1.0, there was tension simmering just under the surface. One wrong move, and somebody would explode.

That someone was Meygan. She lashed out. "Isn't it obvious I need your help right now? Put your stupid phone down already. How many times do I have to ask you!"

Casey stared at her, startled. That's when, maybe for the first time ever, instead of fighting back, he said, "I don't want to keep doing this. I want us to be better." Immediately, Meygan softened. "Me too. I just don't know how." We didn't know how to heal our marriage, but we did know that we couldn't continue carrying on like this.

Of course, the moment wasn't really about the phone or dinner or the crying baby. Because we'd hurt each other so much in the past, Meygan had thought Casey was trying to hurt her again. Why wouldn't she? That behavior would have been par for the course. But Casey's response changed something that day. The argument went from "You always do this" to "Help me understand what hurt you."

By that point in our marriage, the song and dance routine of blowing up and intentionally hurting each other had solidified into a pattern—a habit. One we were now starting to break. You might have come to this book with some bad marriage habits too. One of the phrases we hear all the time from couples is "We're stuck in a rut." That rut could vary from "We watch too many of the same shows" to "We have a screaming match every night" to "We sleep in separate beds." You've both participated in the same behaviors so many times that you've worn those grooves deep and smooth. The problem is not that you've had a thousand fights. It's that you've had the same fight a thousand times. Any time you're triggered or something goes wrong, you fall right back into that bad habit.

Pretty soon, we're going to introduce some new habits into your marriage. But before we dive into the tactical how-to of the book, we want to get you in the right mindset for creating new habits. That's what this chapter is about. Don't panic; there are just two things you need to know. Two very important "rules" we want you to agree to before moving forward.

A healthy mindset comes down to cultivating two traits: curiosity and intentionality. We believe—and have seen in our work with thousands of couples—that these are the two most important characteristics for transforming your marriage. Without them, we experience the slow erosion of connection that leads to frustration, loneliness, and, ultimately, disillusionment.

In the end, only you can fix your marriage. We'll give you the tips and tricks, but without the right mindset overriding it all, even your best attempts to change won't stick. Behavioral transformation is like building a house. None of the fancy and expensive materials you use to build the roof and walls will matter if the foundation crumbles the moment the weather gets bad. Likewise, no marriage tips or coaching or retreats (or even therapy) will work if you do not have the right mindset about your relationship.

GET CURIOUS

In just about every video we record for our app and every coaching session we have with couples, we start with the same piece of advice: Get curious. This is exactly what Meygan's therapist told her to do when we first began repairing our marriage.

When you're dating, you're endlessly curious about your partner. You ask deep questions and find joy in discovering your partner's quirks and dreams. But somewhere along the way—between the kids, the bills, and the demands of everyday life—it's easy to slip into autopilot. You've been together for years. You know a few things about your spouse. You probably even know things you never wanted to know, like what their farts smell like or what sounds they make when they chew. Familiarity can replace the excitement and curiosity of early romance. You stop wondering what's on their mind, what their younger self wanted to be when they grew up, or if they think we need another *Jurassic Park* movie. And you might feel like there is just no sense of mystery anymore. We're willing to bet this is also affecting your sex life, because when we become overly familiar with our spouse, we can lose the sense of intrigue that initially drew us to them. We'll get into more detail about that in a later chapter.

When we screen clients for our marriage intensive program,

this is the main quality we're trying to intuit. Are they curious about themselves, their spouse, and their relationship? Here's one of the most powerful phrases we hear couples say in those interviews: "I don't know why my spouse does that, or why I do that, but I really want to know."

Do you hear how different that sounds from "It's all his/her fault"? Everyone who comes to us for coaching has a list of behaviors they wish their spouse would change. That's normal. Complaints are easy. What's harder, and more powerful, is showing empathy. When you shift from blame to curiosity, you're not pointing fingers anymore. You're saying, "I care enough to try to understand. I'm in this with you." That curiosity shows a willingness to work on it and an open mind to learn.

CASEY'S COACHING CORNER

Curiosity is the on-ramp for empathy and compassion because it shifts our thinking from *What's wrong with them?* to *What hurt are they carrying that I don't see?* When you can see your spouse's perspective, you can much more easily see their struggle.

People are constantly growing and evolving. Yes, you are much more familiar with your partner now than you were before, but there is more to know. Sustaining a healthy marriage requires that you regularly try to see your partner in a new light. Renowned psychotherapist and author Esther Perel says, "Desire needs mystery. . . . It thrives on the mysterious, the novel, and the unexpected. Love is about having; desire is about wanting." Familiarity is inevitable in a long-term relationship, but curiosity helps us see each other as evolving individuals rather than fixed entities. It's the renewal process by which we can rediscover our partner. It counteracts the monotony that often creeps into daily life—the complacency that says, "You bore me. I'm disinterested in you." That's a devastating message that we can send to our spouse without even realizing it.

As we walk through the habits in part 2 of this book, get curious about your feelings and reactions to them. Some tools may be easier or more appealing, and some may seem hard or less attractive to you. Why do you think that is? We aren't therapists, so we aren't here to psychoanalyze you. But we are here to ask you to look inward. Why do you think you have certain beliefs and opinions? Try to withhold judgment for both you and your partner, and just get curious about each other for now.

Here is perhaps the most important thing about curiosity: It shows a sense of humility and openness. When you're curious, you're not on the defensive. You know that there is something you can learn. Improving or changing your marriage will mean doing things you've never done before—breaking old habits and building new ones—and there's always some fumbling along the way as we try new things. That's okay! Try not to take it so seriously. Loosen up your shoulders, relax your jaw, and get a little inquisitive. Curiosity is playful in nature. It's searching and interested and not worried about failing or succeeding.

MEYGAN'S INSIGHT

Because I'm a type A perfectionist, getting curious felt uncomfortable at first because it meant admitting I didn't have all the answers—and that felt vulnerable. But I've learned that curiosity isn't about losing control; it's about letting go of the pressure to be perfect. The shift happens when you realize that progress matters more than polish. Curiosity invites connection, not criticism, and that mindset has changed the way I show up in my marriage.

There is no silver bullet to creating a thriving marriage. But curiosity comes close. It's the ultimate relationship hack. Choose exploration instead of criticism. In that kitchen moment, when Meygan's frustration was boiling over, she could have asked Casey what he was looking at on his phone or what his day was like. Any open-ended question is better than assuming the worst and starting conflict. First, try to gain more information.

As you read through the rest of this book, treat the whole thing like an experiment. We're getting curious about you, your spouse, and your marriage. Which of these habits do you think you'd like to try first? Why? Why do you think you or your partner reacted the way you did to that exercise? No judgment, just curiosity. You are the expert on yourself and your marriage. We're just giving you the tools to cook up the ultimate science experiment and see how good things can get.

BE INTENTIONAL

If curiosity keeps (or reignites) the spark in a relationship, intentionality is the fuel that keeps the fire burning. All it means is that we commit to doing things on purpose. But that commitment is harder to actually practice than it sounds in theory.

Popular author and blogger Michael Hyatt describes something called "the drift," which he connects to a very scary experience he and his wife had while snorkeling. The two of them were celebrating an anniversary at a gorgeous beach in Maui. After some time, Michael came up from under water and realized they'd been caught in a riptide and had drifted far from shore. We experience something similar in our lives and in our marriages. We get so caught up in the day-to-day routine that we accidentally end up in dangerous waters, far away from where we wanted to be. We stopped speaking and acting with intention. And so we've built habits not on purpose but unintentionally, because of the drift. Habits are effective only if you build them consciously, with the idea that they'll lead you where you want to go.

When we talk about being intentional, we mean actively choosing your partner every day, not because it's easy but because it's worth it. That means having a default position of grace instead of judgment, keeping romance alive, speaking kindly instead of critically, and not keeping score of their mistakes. It's the antidote to the myth that great relationships should "flow" naturally. Remember, you *shouldn't* just *know* how to be married. That myth is a recipe for the drift. You have to learn how to be married, practice, and do marriage on purpose. You have to pull your head out of the water, become aware of your current location, and start working toward a new destination.

Intentionality also means being proactive. You can't accomplish anything—from setting a goal to accomplishing a dream to improving your marriage—without being proactive about it. Nothing will happen if you just sit back and wait. It's the difference between saying, "We should go on a date sometime" and actually putting it on the calendar. It's choosing to put your phone down during dinner or writing a quick note of encouragement before your partner's big presentation. These small acts of intention add up, and there is so much power in incremental change over time. It can all start with a single question, like it did for us. Routine is the enemy of connection. It's what turns "How was your day?" into a mindless script instead of a genuine question.

Last, intentionality is a reflection of commitment. If you're not all in and 100 percent committed to giving this a try, you're going to drift. You'll fall back into your old habits, and when the going gets tough, you'll quit. Take it from us, you don't want to do that. Make the intentional choice, every day, to prioritize your partner and your marriage, even in the smallest of ways.

Here's the magic of intentionality and curiosity: They're not just effective individually—they amplify each other for one powerful mindset. Intention sets the direction for your relationship, and curiosity keeps you growing and connecting. You avoid eruptive fights and reactive conflict because you're regularly checking in on your relationship. And instead of making assumptions about why your partner is on their phone or why you're not having sex, you start meaningful and helpful conversations to communicate and get both of your needs met.

We promise, if you can commit to these two traits, you're probably already doing better than 90 percent of couples out there. When people come to us, no matter their issues, if they're willing to get curious and be intentional in their marriage, we know they can make it. If you have curiosity and intentionality, you can change your marriage. And if you can change your marriage, you can change your life.

MEYGAN'S INSIGHT

As you start to cultivate these two traits—curiosity and intentionality—try this exercise. You can do this on a morning walk or during a journaling session. Ask these three connecting questions about yourself and about your marriage:

1. What's working?
2. What's not working?
3. What needs to change?

These questions will pique your curiosity about how you can start to be more intentional with your spouse and in your life.

CONNECTING QUESTIONS

1. Do you consider yourself a curious person often, sometimes, or rarely—and why?

2. What's one thing we could do weekly to feel more connected?

3. How can we be more intentional about prioritizing our marriage no matter how busy life gets?

4. What helps you feel safe enough to be curious in our relationship?

5. What's one area in our marriage where we could be more intentional right now?

6. What's something about me or our marriage you'd like to understand more deeply?

PART II

The Ten Habits

We've ordered the habits in this book from "easiest" to "hardest" to execute. Of course, that's relative and subjective. For some of you, apologizing (the eighth habit) might actually be easier than offering a 60-Second Blessing (the fourth habit). Everyone is different. But this is the sequence we tend to use when we teach the habits in intensives.

These intensives are a focused, two-day experience designed for couples in crisis. They're like emergency care for your relationship where we press pause on all the outside chaos and get serious about healing. We dive deep into core issues and walk through exercises and conversations that rebuild connection and safety. We've done hundreds of them over the last thirteen years, and we've found that it's best to begin with exercises that require the least emotional effort and introspection, before working up to ones that require the most.

Here's why we're telling you this up front. It involves something called the flywheel effect, an idea originated with Jim Collins in his book *Good to Great*. We want you to get some quick wins under your belt. We want you to see an improvement in some aspect of your marriage as fast as possible. Ideally immediately—like, today. Those quick wins and incremental changes will create momentum as you work on other parts of your relationship.

Sometimes, when people feel lost in their marriage and hopeless about how to fix it, they're actually thinking too big. Hurdles like overcoming trauma or righting every wrong you've made in your marriage can feel overwhelming to tackle. Right now, we actually want you to think small. Think about the open-ended question you'll ask her tonight, the coffee you'll make him in the morning, the date you'll plan next week. Think of the movie *What About Bob?*: "Baby steps to get on the bus, baby steps down the aisle. . . ." One good interaction at a time. Create the momentum. Get the flywheel spinning, and the rest—the harder stuff—gets a lot easier.

The KNOWN Position

Because 90 percent of what you're saying ain't coming out of your mouth.

●——————————————————●

Here's a question: Do you know how many times you've looked at your spouse this week? We don't mean glanced in their general direction but actually looked them in the eye. If you're like most couples, it's probably not many. Maybe you're averaging two to four minutes a day of eye contact. You've probably done plenty of things while sitting or standing beside them. We wash the dishes, watch TV, sit at our kids' soccer games, lie in bed, or even go to therapy, and we assume this is enough to make us feel connected.

Being beside each other is better than being on the other side of the house, right? But it's not enough. Proximity is not the same as connection or companionship. Just because you're beside each other doesn't mean you're *with* each other, *seeing* each other. We live in a distraction-driven culture. It's easy to be in the same room but not truly be present with your spouse. You might share a home, but if you're not sharing attention, you're not connected. Attention is how we feel known and important. It's a form of love. And the best way to pay attention is to look someone in the eye.

This first marriage habit is all about looking at each other, on purpose. It's about being seen. The technique we're about to share has transformed hundreds of marriages during our intensives and retreats. We call it the KNOWN position. It's a framework we developed to help couples communicate with incredible intentionality. At its core, it works to meet a universal need in all relationships: to know and be known.

That's what we all want, isn't it? Marriage isn't about doing life disconnected or alone. It's about showing up for each other, creating a safe space to explore fears, insecurities, dreams, and joys. When couples come to us in crisis, they describe feeling unseen, unheard, and invalidated whenever they're together. This disconnection drives them apart. They don't feel *known*. And being known means being fully seen. So that's where we start.

Truly seeing someone means accepting them—their essence, their fears, and their hopes. When someone feels known, they feel valued, significant, and meaningful. They know they are safe, even in their messiness and vulnerability. It means security in the relationship. But achieving this level of connection takes intentionality. It's not something that happens in passing, without effort. You communicate that someone is important to you with deliverance and thoughtfulness. You look at them—really see them—in all their messiness and love them anyway.

Research from UCLA psychology professor Albert Mehrabian suggests that 55 percent of communication comes through body language. To quote Will Smith's character in the cinematic classic rom-com *Hitch*, "Sixty percent of all human communication is nonverbal . . . 30 percent is your tone. So that means that 90 percent of what you're saying—ain't coming out of your mouth." Things like eye contact and open body postures contribute greatly to what you're communicating to your spouse. If you never look at them, never face them, or are never physically close to them, you don't have to use words to communicate that you're feeling distant or pissed. They already know. Even if you're not actually disinterested or upset, that's what you're communicating.

That's where the KNOWN position comes in. We came up with this technique years ago at a marriage intensive. Originally, during sessions, we'd have our clients sit side by side on the couch. But one day, during a particularly powerful session with a couple who were apologizing to each other for some deep hurts, we had the idea to sit them right in front of each other. We noticed that they both kept squirming a little, twisting away from each other. It was almost as if the connection felt like too much. But we knew how important it was that they heard and understood each other and communicated that with their bodies. So we put them in what we now call the KNOWN position. KNOWN is an acronym that stands for the following:

- **K**nee-to-knee
- **N**o distractions
- **O**pen body language
- **W**hole self
- **N**urturing eye contact

We didn't want them to turn away. We didn't want them to miss this powerful moment just because they were uncomfortable with the intimacy. After we realized how effective this was, we named it, created a process, and started incorporating it into all our marriage intensives and into coaching. We don't want our retreats to be a time when couples only face us up on a stage and hear us cheer them on and give some good advice. On day one, we have them all turn their chairs and get into the KNOWN position. This is when the magic happens.

Remember that 2010 exhibition *The Artist Is Present*? For nearly three months in New York's Museum of Modern Art (MoMA), Serbian conceptual artist Marina Abramović sat for hours on end as she made prolonged eye contact with strangers. People waited in line for a chance to sit with her. Some wept, some laughed, and some gazed intimately for thirty minutes or more. Many participants said the experience changed their lives. The KNOWN position works in a similar way. We use it regularly ourselves, and we instruct couples to try it when they're exploring something especially important or painful. We've even experimented with it in times when we just needed five minutes of uninterrupted eye contact. You don't have to go that far if you don't want to, but sitting in the KNOWN position and trying for just one minute of eye contact might show you how rare it is these days to look hard at your spouse without a distraction.

Whether it's with a stranger at MoMA or your partner of twenty years, eye contact—and open body language in general—is undeniably a key to connection. So before we ask you to change any of your behaviors in your marriage or say anything to your spouse, we're going to teach you how to just look at them, be with them, and make them feel known. Let's break it down.

KNEE-TO-KNEE

Physical proximity matters. When we're knee-to-knee, we're intentionally creating a space for connection, and obviously, we're very close to each other. It's intimate and present. Sitting side by side doesn't work as well—we're not fully facing each other. In the KNOWN position, our knees touch, and even in something as small as this, we signal that we are fully here for each other. Practically, it allows for a partner to lay a hand on the other's leg for encouragement, to reach out to wipe away a tear, or to lean in for a hug.

CASEY'S COACHING CORNER

Physical closeness helps regulate the nervous system and reminds you and your partner that you're on the same team—the two of you are not enemies. It's surprisingly hard to yell or stay defensive when you're looking at each other and can literally feel one another's presence. This posture encourages empathy, safety, and emotional engagement, which helps keep the conversation respectful and connected.

NO DISTRACTIONS

Distractions kill intentional communication. So many couples miss the opportunity for healthy communication because they're trying to talk while watching TV, staring at their phones, cooking dinner, or doing any of the other day-to-day activities that consume our time. We live in a culture where just about every device is trying to get us to pay attention with a quick dopamine hit. It's a recipe for missing something important that your spouse is trying to tell you, or failing to pick up on those all-important nonverbal cues. In the KNOWN position, the TV is off, phones are out of sight, and the kids are in another room. By eliminating distractions, you're telling your partner, "You are my priority right now." For couples in which one or both partners have ADHD (Casey: *Hi, that's us!*), minimizing background noise is critical. Casey loves having music on, but during our KNOWN time, we've agreed to turn it off or keep it barely audible because it's distracting for Meygan. If you absolutely must have something on, pick some classical or spa music. Make sure nothing gets in the way of you giving each other your full, shared attention.

OPEN BODY LANGUAGE

When you cross your arms or legs, or lean back in your chair, it can convey defensiveness or disinterest. Open body language— uncrossed arms, facing forward—says, "I'm open to you." It's a small shift that makes a big difference in how your partner feels during a conversation or interaction. For women especially, crossing your legs might feel natural, but it can unintentionally communicate that you are emotionally closed off. If you're wearing a dress and are worried about flashing your partner, you can keep your legs closed, but try not to cross them. (Then again, if you want to make your connection time a little more interesting . . . maybe go right ahead and flash him. That's one way to signal you'd like to "connect" later.)

WHOLE SELF

Hopefully you're now physically communicating that you're present and open, but you have to mean it mentally as well. (You committed to being all in when you read the last chapter, remember?) Don't sit there thinking about the kids, work, or household tasks. Focus entirely on the moment and your partner. Like Ron Swanson says in a *Parks and Recreation* episode, "Never half-ass two things. Whole-ass one thing." When you're with your partner, be all there.

Honesty and vulnerability are key here. Share your real thoughts, feelings, and fears. If your spouse works late every night and it bothers you, don't say, "It's fine, I know you're busy" when you really mean you're hurt and lonely and fear you're not a priority anymore. Don't brush off hard truths simply to avoid conflict. Resentment will build, and nothing will change. Let your spouse hear your authentic thoughts and feelings. For example, "I've been feeling lonely with how often you're working late. And I'm worried our relationship is taking a back seat to your job."

In a later chapter, we'll talk more about how to have these kinds of conversations and what you might be doing in the KNOWN position (any of the subsequent nine habits!). But suffice it to say, whatever is going on while you're looking at each other, be all there.

MEYGAN'S INSIGHT

I get it—our minds never really stop. We're tracking the kids' schedules, what's for dinner, the next dentist appointment, and that broken doorknob no one else seems to notice. That mental load is real, and it's heavy. But when it's time to connect with your spouse, you've got to consciously set the load down for a moment. You deserve to be fully present, and so does your marriage. This connection time isn't just another task—it's the fuel that helps everything else run better.

NURTURING EYE CONTACT

Joy Hirsch, a neuroscientist at Yale School of Medicine and founder of the school's Brain Function Laboratory, says that our brains have a way of synchronizing during eye contact. "They become kind of phase-locked in a coherent state," she explains. With sustained eye contact, the electrical rhythms in our brains start to align—they literally get on the same wavelength. It's as if your brain is tuning in to your partner's frequency, creating a shared neural experience that boosts empathy, understanding, and connection. Your eyes are, quite literally, a gateway to emotional intimacy.

Eye contact is deeply vulnerable and incredibly powerful. But we added *nurturing* to the acronym not only because, let's be honest, we needed an *N*, but also because we want your gaze to communicate love and attention. It's not a quick glance or a stare-down. It's a warm invitation for connection and belonging. This step is not just a requirement that you look—it's about *how* you look. If you're not used to eye contact, you'll be tempted to look away. Or worse, to look as annoyed as you might feel. At the very least, try to keep your gaze neutral. As you do this, and the other habits, it will become easier to make eye contact. Feeling awkward at the beginning is normal. But that's not an excuse not to try.

If you're struggling, gently focus on your partner's eyes. Casey has been (fairly) called out for staring at Meygan's boobs once or twice during this exercise. He's only human. If you're having trouble focusing, try to pick just one of your spouse's eyes and look into the pupil (that's the black part if it's been a minute since you studied eye anatomy). Pick a pupil, stare, and see what happens. We promise it's more powerful than you think.

Bonus tip: If you're really feeling it, you could hold hands. Holding hands isn't necessary, but it deepens the intimacy and can be very moving if you haven't held your spouse's hand in a while. When we drift emotionally, it tends to happen physically too. So think about adding a hand-holding to this technique if it feels right.

PRACTICAL APPLICATION

When we sit in the KNOWN position, we're fully present for each other, which is the first step in creating a healthy marriage. This position is especially effective for people who have physical touch as a love language (see: Casey Caston). In our intensives, we've seen couples sit like this for hours reconnecting. It's emotional and healing. We've had countless people tell us that it was the first time they'd felt seen by their partner in years, sometimes even decades. Most of them didn't talk about anything especially deep. They just looked at each other for the first time in a long time.

So, when do you actually use the KNOWN position? The short answer is: anytime you want. You can't really overuse it—unless you've stopped parenting or working or eating and are staring at each other for ten hours a day. Then you've overdone it. Basically, the KNOWN position is a foundation for any of the other habits we're going to discuss. It's like the sweetener or accelerant that makes every other habit more effective. For example, you can use it for the following situations:

1. *Rebuilding trust:* If you've broken trust, you can use the KNOWN position as a safe space to have those hard, emotional conversations.

2. *Repair attempts:* Use this technique during apologies or discussions about past hurts.

3. *Difficult topics:* For issues that tend to escalate into fights, start the conversation in the KNOWN position. We promise you'll find it much harder to fight when you're in this vulnerable, open state.

4. *Daily connection:* Even when things are good, use this position to deepen your bond. It's not just for crisis moments. Use it for the 60-Second Blessing or even the Weekly Marriage Business Meeting. More on those later.

The intentionality of the KNOWN position makes it perfect for addressing heated topics, whether it's finances, in-laws, or past conflicts. When emotions run high, this posture reminds you to focus on connection rather than winning an argument. And when you just want to have a normal conversation or offer a compliment, this position makes those positive experiences even better.

HOW TO GET STARTED

To ask your spouse to get in the KNOWN position, simply say, "Can we sit knee-to-knee?" Set aside a distraction-free space and time. If you're nervous, start small—use it for a quick check-in at the end of your day. As you get comfortable, expand its use to longer, deeper conversations.

MEYGAN'S INSIGHT

If you're really hurting in your marriage and the KNOWN position feels too intimate or unsafe for you right now, just try one or two letters. Work on using more open body language or nurturing eye contact in small doses. Limit your distractions when you're with your partner or focus on bringing your whole self to your conversations, even if they're minimal right now. Even these small, incremental efforts will compound and make a difference. It's okay to work your way up to the whole position.

The KNOWN position isn't just a technique; it's a mindset. It's about showing up fully for your partner and creating a space where both of you can be understood and appreciated. You each have a place, a say, and value in this relationship. When we first started using it, we realized how disconnected we'd been, even when sitting on the same couch. Now it's our go-to method for meaningful communication.

Casey is an experienced (and super fun) wedding officiant and has done well over a thousand weddings. As someone who frequently gets to witness a couple on the first day of their marriage as they stand and say their vows, he knows there's a reason why we face each other at that moment—open, engaged, loved, ready. When we pledge our lives to each other, for better or worse, we're in the KNOWN position. Maybe not knee-to-knee, but as close as you can get while standing. No distractions, open body language, whole self, nurturing eye contact, holding hands.

Every couple that we work with meant those vows when they

said them, whether it was last year or fifty years ago. They meant them deeply. If you did too, and you're wondering how to get back to that place of feeling loved and known, we encourage you to start here. We cannot overstate the power of this position. See each other. Be with each other. Don't put any more pressure on it than that.

CONNECTING QUESTIONS

1. Are you willing to try to use the KNOWN position the next time we talk about something important? Why or why not?

2. How does it feel when we make eye contact with each other?

3. What are some distractions that can get in the way of us having a conversation? How can we limit those distractions so we can sit in the KNOWN position?

4. Is there any kind of nonverbal communication or physical touch that you want me to stay away from? Why?

5. What are some topics we may want to consider discussing in the KNOWN position?

The Weekly Marriage Business Meeting

Get back on the same team (and page).

•————————————————————•

One of the most common phrases we hear when people first join Marriage365 or come to one of our intensives is "I just don't feel like we're on the same page." Have you ever felt like that?

Once Meygan had been looking forward to a relaxing Friday night at home all week long. It had been a tough week, and all she wanted to do was snuggle on the couch and binge-watch a show. But—little problem—she didn't communicate that to Casey. So Casey invited two other couples over for dinner that night, last minute. He knew Meygan had been missing hanging out with people and thought she'd be excited to host. (Casey: *Admittedly, giving her a little heads-up would have been good.*)

At six-thirty Meygan walked into the kitchen in sweatpants. Casey said, "Babe! They'll be here in thirty minutes!" There was no food prepped, the house was a wreck, and mentally, Meygan was not prepared to talk for the next few hours. We did the classic "run around the house and shove everything into a closet" move and ordered pizza. Problem solved. But still, Meygan was frustrated, and Casey spent the whole night feeling like a failure.

In the midst of our busy lives, this is what happens all too often, isn't it? We get so bogged down in the day-to-day that we just miss each other. We walk past and go about our business with zero idea of what the other person is doing, feeling, thinking about, planning. Marriage can feel like a constant game of catch-up. At times we have felt like we were two overworked employees trying to run a family without a game plan. And because we never *actually* sat down to discuss what was happening, we ended up in ridiculous fights about who was supposed to pay a bill or who should be where on what night.

A study originally by the UCLA Sloan Center, then highlighted by John Gottman of the Gottman Institute, found that the average couple spends less than thirty-five minutes per week talking in a purposeful way. None of this is happening because we don't love each other, of course. It is happening because we aren't aligned. We're making assumptions instead of agreements. We're being reactive instead of proactive. The worst part about this misalignment—way worse than missing an appointment or having to unexpectedly order pizza instead of home-cooking a meal—is that it translates into every single part of your marriage. It affects your conversations, your sex life, your connection, how you respond to crises, and how you support each other every single day.

In 2024 we polled our audience, and more than twelve thousand people responded to the question "What happens when you and your spouse actually schedule time together?" The top answer was "We feel more connected and in sync." And the second was "It helps us communicate better and fight less."

So, after struggling for years and feeling like we weren't on the same page in multiple ways, we had an epiphany. We had no problem planning our work schedules, taxes, vacations, doctor visits, teeth cleanings, school events, birthday parties, and so much more. Why weren't we planning our marriage? Think about it—in just about every area of life, it's completely normal and necessary to have a "business meeting." (How many soul-draining work meetings have you been in that could have easily been an email?) We have regular meetings with our kids' teachers, team coaches, HOA assemblies, PTA boards, accountants, etc. We instinctively know that planning is a big part of success. So why do we do so little planning for our marriages? We think it goes back to the myths. We're supposed to know how to do this. If we're really in love, it'll just "work out."

In intensives, when we ask couples what they've done so far to work on their marriage, they often say they haven't done much. One or both partners just kept hoping that things would get better. Hear this loud and clear: *Hope is not a strategy.* Intentionality is. Do not run your marriage on hope. Get proactive and intentional about it. Eventually, we built a structured, proactive way to align our week—and it changed everything. It's called the Weekly Marriage Business Meeting (WMBM).

First, we're going to ask you to do something that might seem too simple: Sync your digital calendars. In fact, at our intensives, it's one of the very first practices we have couples do. If you're a paper calendar kind of person (looking at you, hardcore daily planner ladies), that's okay. But we HIGHLY recommend also using a digital calendar that you sync with your partner and keep updated. There are plenty of apps these days that can sync calendars without you having to do it manually. There's more to this habit than just that, which we'll get into in a bit. But that's the first and perhaps most important part. Time is your most precious nonrenewable resource. You and your partner need to be on the same page about how you're spending it.

In 2024 we polled five hundred Marriage365 members and asked them which of our resources they felt like they couldn't live without. Nearly three-fourths (71 percent) answered the Weekly Marriage Business Meeting worksheet, which is the tool we're going to talk about in this chapter. You can download it for free on our website if you want to mark it up (Marriage365Books .com/resources).

After teaching this system to tens of thousands of couples, we've consistently heard the same feedback:

- "This cut our fighting in half."
- "We finally feel like a team again."
- "I didn't realize how much I was assuming instead of communicating."

If you've ever found yourself in an argument that started with "I thought you were picking up the kids" or "Wait, you're going to the doctor now?!" or even "I had no idea you were going through that; why didn't you tell me?"—congratulations, you're married. And we get it. Life is busy. Between work, kids, social obligations, and that never-ending pile of laundry, it feels impossible to slow down and have an intentional conversation. But when couples don't communicate *proactively*, they communicate reactively. And reactive communication tends to sound like this:

- "Why didn't you tell me about this?"
- "I thought you were handling it."
- "You spent HOW MUCH on Amazon?"

That's where the WMBM comes in. Yes, we know. The name sounds about as romantic as filing your taxes, but trust us—this simple thirty-to-sixty-minute check-in will change your marriage. Sound good? We thought so. Let's break it down.

The Weekly Marriage Business Meeting is a weekly meeting (duh) in which you and your partner go over six recurring topics and answer three simple questions. We do ours on Sunday to look at the week ahead. If you have kids and busy jobs, this might take you sixty minutes. If you have a light week, it might be closer to thirty. And you certainly don't have to do it on Sundays. Find whatever night of the week works for you.

This isn't just about logistics—it's about you. It's a chance to reconnect, recalibrate, and ensure you're prioritizing your marriage, not just coexisting under the same roof. It's also a chance to see what the other person has on their plate and offer support. In this chapter, we'll unpack the six topics we want you to cover each week. You could even print out the worksheet or laminate it and write on it with dry-erase markers. Regardless of how you use it, staying in sync on these topics will transform your relationship.

CASEY'S COACHING CORNER

From one husband to another, this is one habit that 95 percent of the men I work with don't have any trouble getting behind. It's about planning and logistics, which most of us enjoy. But it also means we make sure the fun stuff (sex) happens too. Things don't usually get too stressful. Initiate the WMBM. I promise, you'll become husband of the year.

MEYGAN'S INSIGHT

Wives, listen up. Husbands love the WMBM. If there's one habit you can get them on board with, it's this. It's a great one to start with. The best part is that once you get all this scheduling stuff out of the way, you don't have to address it again, and it leaves time to connect the rest of the week.

---

1. SCHEDULES:
WHO'S DOING WHAT, WHERE, AND WHEN?

Marriage is a team sport, and teams don't win games without game plans. After you've synced your calendars, it's time for your first business meeting. Pull out your phones or tablets and go through the week ahead. Ask these questions:

- Who's picking up the kids?
- Who has late meetings?
- When do we have time together?
- Are there any social events we've forgotten about?

The point of this part is pretty obvious: Go over your upcoming calendars so nothing falls through the cracks and everyone knows what's going on and what their responsibilities are. You'd be amazed at how many couples simply don't know what's on each other's plate for work, kids, hobbies, and friendships.

Once, before we were doing these WMBMs, Casey knew he had to take our son, Cordell, to therapy. But because we didn't have clear and synced calendars, he took him to occupational therapy instead of speech therapy. Meygan got a call from the speech therapist wondering where he was and a call from the occupational therapist saying he wasn't on the calendar but since he was there they could squeeze him in. Meygan was panicking, of course, and couldn't get ahold of Casey because he was in a meeting. She was so mad at him, which led to an argument later that evening. The WMBM eliminates this kind of miscommunication and any resulting conflict.

2. BUDGETS:
LET'S TALK MONEY (WITHOUT FIGHTING)

Money stress doesn't come from not having enough. It comes from not knowing where it's going. The second box to check during your WMBM is your budget. We do a quick financial check-in so there are no "Wait . . . how much did we spend this month!" moments. This includes the following:

- What's coming in and what's going out?
- Are there big expenses we need to plan for?
- Do we need to rein in spending this week?

One month, Casey needed new tires ($1,000) and Meygan had an unexpected dental bill ($500). Had we not discussed finances, it would've been one of those "Why didn't we plan for this!" situations. Instead, we adjusted our spending *before* it became an issue. No fighting, no hiding, no miscommunication, no shame.

After you've synced your schedules, go over what bills or expenses are coming up so you can plan for them. Here's a caveat: We know from reporting from Ramsey Solutions that nearly 48 percent of couples with significant debt say money is a top reason for arguments in their relationship. If this is a much bigger issue for you, the kind that can't be resolved in a few minutes during your WMBM, you might need outside help. If it's regularly causing fights or impeding the progress of this weekly meeting, you might even want to remove it. That's totally fine. The purpose of this practice is to get on the same page. If one of these six topics is pushing you even further apart, it's okay to remove it until you get more help.

3. SELF-CARE:
YOU CAN'T POUR FROM AN EMPTY CUP

Raise your hand if you've ever felt burned-out, exhausted, and like you have nothing left to give. We can't see you, but we're going to assume every single one of you can identify with that statement. In this day and age, burnout is common. And it affects marriages too. Marriage isn't just about showing up for your partner—it's about showing up as the best version of yourself.

It takes two healthy people to make a marriage. You can't show up as a good spouse if you're burned-out. So during this part of the WMBM we ask each other these questions:

- "What's an area of self-care you want to focus on this week?"
- "How can I support your self-care without guilt?"

Self-care is anything that recharges, re-energizes, or refreshes you. It offers you rest and makes you feel grounded and relaxed so you can be present for the people who matter most. It's not just about bubble baths, although it certainly can be. All that matters is that it helps you be the best version of yourself. It could be any of the following:

- Time at the gym
- A nap (seriously, sometimes that's all we need)
- A night out with friends
- Stretching
- Journaling
- Praying
- Reading a book
- A walk around the block
- Turning off phone notifications for the day
- Taking a drive with no agenda
- Dancing/singing to your favorite song

We all practice self-care in different ways. Meygan often needs a solo coffee date to recharge, while Casey needs a surf session. When we respect each other's needs, though, we show up better for each other. And planning out our self-care is way better than asking for it in the moment when we need it. By then, we're already overwhelmed or overstimulated, and the ask won't be as well received by our partner. Do not neglect yourself, and encourage your partner to prioritize their well-being also.

4. CONNECTION TIME:
ARE WE ACTUALLY SEEING EACH OTHER?

Remember how we said the average couple spends under thirty-five minutes together alone in meaningful conversation? Yeah, that's not good. The next step in the WMBM is to make sure you're getting some connection time each week.

This doesn't have to be a date night. It's great if it is, but for many couples, whether it's for financial or life reasons, going out each week isn't feasible. Sometimes resentment or hurt builds up and hours of quality one-on-one time become uncomfortable. It's easier to stay distracted or busy to avoid that intimacy. Other times it's simply the mental load and exhaustion of everyday life that get in the way. That all makes sense and can be used as a reason not to spend quality time together. Maybe start with something simpler and shorter. Fifteen minutes here and there—a less vulnerable way to engage. Here are some ideas:

- Have couch time together without phones
- Do morning coffee check-ins
- Read a book together
- Listen to a podcast together or listen separately and talk about it together
- Pull out old photo albums
- Walk the dog
- Send funny memes or TikTok videos
- Give each other five-minute massages
- Dance in the kitchen to your favorite song
- Do a puzzle
- Do the *New York Times* crossword
- Do a house project together
- Take a stroll through a park
- Go through *365 Connecting Questions*
- Play a card game
- Play a board game
- Take a drive

See? Connection time isn't just about dates or spending money. It's time when you're together—doing something together—that doesn't revolve around kids, work, or logistics. There are so many ideas other than what's on our list. The sky's the limit, and every couple is different. But the point is you do have to schedule this time, every single week. However much you want is up to you. We recommend starting with fifteen minutes three times a week. If you've come to this book wondering how to get back to that fun-loving, relaxed couple you used to be who always had unlimited time for each other, this is a great way to start.

MEYGAN'S INSIGHT

Connection in marriage should be a shared responsibility, not something only one person carries. Otherwise, resentment can build. When both spouses take turns initiating connection time, it sends the message "You matter to me." Healthy marriages are built on effort from both sides, not just one person doing all the reaching.

---

5. MEAL PLANNING:
WHAT ARE WE GOING TO EAT?

Okay, we know this might not seem like a big deal, but meal planning is important—especially when life gets busy. And the reality is that the average family can save over $1,500 a year if they meal plan. If you're on a budget and are already exhausted because of normal life, experiencing decision fatigue as you stare aimlessly into the fridge at six o'clock wondering what to eat is not a recipe for feeling connected and calm with your spouse. Meal planning will cut down on your expenses and the conflict with your spouse during those hectic, busy weeknights.

If money isn't an issue, then by all means, get takeout or delivery. The point is to cut down on last-minute decision-making and any potential frustrations. And to assign who is responsible for it so there's no blaming. We end up driving to Chick-fil-A plenty of nights when the kids have sports. There's no shame in that. But we try to know ahead of time that that's what we're doing, so we're not left scrambling at the last minute. We've even gotten into the habit of putting what we're eating each day in our shared calendar.

If you feel like meal planning isn't something that applies to you or your marriage, you can skip or replace this part of the meeting. For us, this was a source of contention early in our marriage because Meygan hates to cook and Casey loves to eat. And in our work with couples, we've found that sorting out meals, specifically dinners, helps the most overwhelmed and busy people minimize stress and decision fatigue, in addition to saving money and helping with financial goals.

6. SEXY TIME:
YEP, WE'RE GOING THERE

We know. Scheduling sex? That doesn't sound exciting! That's not how it is in the movies! "This isn't the spontaneous 'push me up against the door in the middle of the day' sex life I was promised!" Believe us, we've heard those objections hundreds of times. But this is real life. To be clear, we're all for pushing your partner up against the door in the middle of the day if you know they'd be into that. But that's just not the reality for most couples. Most weeks we're slammed at work, or the kids are home, or we are scheduled to the max every single night. Sure, scheduling sex might not sound exciting. But you know what's even *less* exciting? Not having sex.

CASEY'S COACHING CORNER

Boy, do we get a lot of guff about scheduling sex and how it takes all the romance out of it. And I completely disagree. Here's a conversation we've never had after having scheduled sex: "Boy, that was a waste of time; I mean, I didn't feel anything special here." No. In fact, we feel grateful that we prioritized it enough to make it happen.

So yes, we put it on the calendar. And we challenge you to try this and tell us with a straight face that anticipating sex all day isn't that sexy. Go ahead. We'll wait. We've been doing this for more than fifteen years and haven't met a person yet who reports that scheduling sex took all the fun out of it. *The Journal of Sex Research* found that while many individuals believe spontaneous sex is more satisfying, there is no significant difference in satisfaction between spontaneous and planned sexual encounters.

Before we did this in our own marriage, we'd have weeks where we'd say, "We should have sex soon." And then, boom— it'd be two weeks later, and we'd forgotten to prioritize intimacy. For us, it's Wednesday nights. (The *real* hump day.) Our kids go to youth group, the house is empty, and that's our time. And guess what? It works. Casey is extra attentive during the day as a form of foreplay. And because she knows it's coming, Meygan gets to anticipate sex and prepare, which many women enjoy. Scheduling sex isn't about *taking out the spontaneity*—it's about making sure intimacy happens at all.

So schedule it! We recommend at least once a week, though by all means, schedule it as often as you'd like. In our schedule we call it NAP time (Naughty and Playful) since sometimes our teenagers get a glimpse of the calendar. If finding time for intimacy has been a struggle, try putting it on the calendar and see what happens.

BEFORE YOU CLOSE

All right, those are the basics. Now, here is the nitty-gritty. At the end of your Weekly Marriage Business Meeting, we want you to ask each other three questions.

1. What is something I can do to help you this week?

This is a show of support for your spouse. We've found that most people's answers aren't even major asks. They're things like "Ask me how my day was" or "Watch a show with me on Thursday" or "Pick up the kids on Wednesday so I can go to dinner with the girls." The answer might even be "Nothing," which is also okay. Simply asking shows that you're on each other's team. You're in this together. And you care about each other's well-being and workload. This may be especially important for a spouse to ask the stay-at-home parent who often gets overlooked because they don't work outside of the house. They still need support, perhaps more than anyone. Try to take on one thing to help each other out this week.

2. How can we prioritize our relationship this week?

You might have already answered this one when you planned for connection time, but it's okay to reiterate it here or think of something else. This is a check to ensure your marriage doesn't get put on the back burner when things get busy.

3. Are there any concerns, stresses, or worries you have for the coming week?

This question allows you to address any potential issues proactively before they escalate. It also opens the door for emotional connection. Maybe you have a big meeting at work that you're worried about. Maybe you have a phone call that you're dreading or a doctor's appointment that's making you nervous. Let your spouse in on that. Let them carry it with you. This allows them to support you and follow up. It also helps you feel not alone in your worries. If necessary, perhaps your spouse can even trouble-shoot or game-plan with you.

Reflecting on these three questions, and the topics covered in the WMBM, is one of the best and simplest ways to reconnect

Weekly Marriage Business Meeting

- [ ] 🗓 Schedules
- [ ] ☁ Self-Care
- [ ] 🍽 Meal Plans
- [ ] _____

- [ ] 💲 Budget
- [ ] ♡ Connection Time
- [ ] 👄 Sexy Time
- [ ] _____

💬 What is something I can do to help you this week?

💬 How can we prioritize our relationship this week?

💬 Are there any concerns, stresses, or worries you have for the coming week?

in your marriage and reduce conflict. Try it out this week. Sync your digital calendars and schedule a WMBM. Then walk through each item and watch your lives quickly get back on the same page.

●━━━━━━━━━━━━━━━●

CONNECTING QUESTIONS

1. How do you feel about the balance between work, family, and personal time right now? Do we need to make any changes?

2. What nights do we want to eat together without screens or distractions?

3. What would be the best time and day for us to do the Weekly Marriage Business Meeting?

4. What's something fun or meaningful we can plan for just the two of us this week so we can have connection time?

5. What does practicing self-care look like for you, is this something you struggle with, and why?

Love Lists

The cheat sheet for loving your spouse well.

———————————————•——————————————————•

Not long ago, Meygan was on a walk with one of her dear friends. This friend has five children and, as you can imagine, a very full life. She's been married for many years now, but she told Meygan that she'd been feeling more and more disconnected from her husband lately.

"He's so incredibly helpful," she said. "He's constantly doing things around the house, taking the kids places, and trying to take tasks off my plate. I know he loves me and he's trying to show it by doing things for our family. I don't mean to sound ungrateful, but I just wish he'd talk to me more. I'd rather him reassure me that I'm doing a good job than have him load the dishwasher one more time."

Conversely, in another couple that we coached, the husband was a fire captain. He worked long shifts and didn't have a normal nine-to-five schedule. When he came back from a stretch of being gone for two to three days, all he wanted to do was sit down on the couch and talk with his wife. But she'd been home all that time with the kids and wanted help with meals and changing lightbulbs and getting the kids to soccer games. He would try to start a long conversation about everything that happened while they'd been apart. This, unfortunately, was in direct conflict with what she wanted—which was to take a long bubble bath and not speak to anyone for at least an hour.

In both examples, nobody was in the wrong. That's the first thing to acknowledge. All the desires and expectations of these four individuals were incredibly normal and valid. But they completely missed each other, right? All four individuals wanted love and connection from a spouse, but they were offering and receiving it in conflicting ways. In our marriage intensives, we hear over and over again that one person is always saying, "I love you" or giving foot rubs or doing the laundry or (maybe the most common) working hard to pay the bills, and yet their partner doesn't "feel" loved. This leads to one or both partners feeling like their effort wasn't enough.

All of us want to be loved. And all of us want to love our spouse, right? If you've picked up this book, hopefully we don't have to try to convince you of that. But the enduring popularity of Gary Chapman's *The 5 Love Languages* highlights that this is still a struggle for most of us. Chapman coined five types of love languages: words of affirmation, acts of service, receiving gifts, quality time, and physical touch. Recently, psychologists and relationship coaches have argued that love is a lot more nuanced. Some people feel loved through shared experiences, deep conversations, or space and independence. Even food can be a love language. What makes love tricky, as illustrated by the two aforementioned couples, is that most of us fall into a rut of loving our spouse the way we want to be loved, and vice versa.

To solve this, we came up with something called Love Lists. While the love languages concept gives you a general understanding of your partner's preferences, Love Lists take it a step further by finding über-specific, actionable ways to meet those preferences. It's a powerful activity for helping you eliminate the guesswork and clearly communicate how you and your partner want to be loved.

Each spouse writes down ten to twenty specific, positive ways their partner can show love—no vague answers allowed. Think "Text me during the day to say you're thinking of me" instead of "Be more romantic." Then you exchange lists and walk away with a personalized cheat sheet on how to love your partner well. It's simple and practical, and it removes assumptions so you can start meeting each other's needs with confidence and clarity. It's like SparkNotes for your relationship. These lists aren't about grand gestures (though those are nice) but about the small, meaningful actions that make a big difference day-to-day.

CASEY'S COACHING CORNER

I hear a lot of guys complain that they're putting all this effort into their marriage but rarely get credit. Love Lists are about becoming more efficient in your relationships. Stop wasting energy by putting your love in all the wrong places.

When we first got married, Meygan would sometimes drop hints, make comments, and then get frustrated when Casey didn't pick up on them. (Sound familiar, ladies?) She'd mention more than once how much she just *loved* flowers and *adored* the cappuccinos from the coffee shop down the road. But alas, no flowers or coffee turned up unexpectedly on a Tuesday. On the flip side, Casey assumed Meygan wanted to be loved in the same way he did, which led to a lot of effort on his part (to have sex) that didn't quite land. Over time, resentment crept in. We loved each other, but we often felt disconnected, like trains running on different tracks.

That's when we decided to stop guessing. We sat down and created our first set of Love Lists. These lists gave us a simple, clear way to articulate exactly how we wanted to be loved—and it changed everything. We've seen this play out in countless other marriages. One husband shared how he'd been buying his wife flowers regularly, only to find out through her Love List that she valued acts around the house far more. When he switched to unloading the dishwasher and prepping meals instead, she felt more loved than ever. This was shocking news to him, and a simple fix.

Real love is about choice. It's choosing to love in the way our spouse likes to receive it, even if it's not the way we like to be loved. A Love List helps us close this gap by offering clarity and intention.

In this chapter, we're going to walk you through how Love Lists work, why they're effective, and how they can transform your marriage. Too many people feel unappreciated because their efforts to express love don't align with their partner's needs. It's like a stationary bike—lots of effort, but you're going nowhere. If that statement resonates with you, we're about to fix that. There's a better way.

HERE'S HOW IT WORKS

1. Set aside time to individually create your lists. This can take anywhere from fifteen minutes to an hour.

2. Write down ten to twenty specific things your spouse can do to make you feel loved. Take the time you need.

3. Exchange your lists, read them together, and discuss.

4. Use your lists as a guide to intentionally love each other. Throughout the week, pick one thing on the list and do it.

Sounds simple, right? It is—but don't underestimate its power. And don't breeze over the exercise. When making your Love Lists, keep these guidelines in mind:

1. *Be specific.* Vague requests like "help out more" won't cut it. Instead, be detailed: "Unload the dishwasher after dinner on weeknights."

2. *Make them positive.* Avoid phrasing items as "don'ts." Instead of "Don't interrupt me," say, "Ask me clarifying questions during our conversations."

3. *Be realistic.* Your requests should fit your life circumstances. If you're both juggling demanding jobs and three kids, "Plan a surprise trip to Hawaii" might not be feasible right now.

4. *Keep it measurable.* Choose actions that are clear and doable. For example, instead of saying, "Love me more," try "Give me a thirty-second hug every day."

You can get our Love List template at Marriage365Books .com/resources. One for you and one for your spouse. Start by reflecting on these questions:

- What actions make me feel loved and appreciated?
- What words or gestures brighten my day?
- What are the little things my spouse has done in the past that made me feel connected? (If you're struggling with ideas, think back to when you were dating. Did your partner do anything back then that really did it for you?)
- What have others done that made me feel appreciated?

- What small interaction that might have happened years ago still makes me happy when I think about it today?

Here are some examples to inspire you, categorized by ways people receive love. To be clear, you do not need to know your love language to create a Love List. Plenty of our clients don't. But this will give you a feel for what different kinds of specific, action-oriented, clear Love List items can look like.

If you love words:

- Tell me you're proud of me when I accomplish something.
- Leave me a handwritten sticky note on my desk.
- Compliment me in front of another person.
- Tell me "I love you" while we're in the car.
- Praise me when you see me working hard at something.
- Text me while you're at work and let me know you're thinking about me.
- Tell me you appreciate how hard I work for this family.

If you love actions:

- Make dinner once a week without me asking.
- Clean up the backyard with the kids on Saturday mornings.
- Get up with the kids and let me sleep in.
- Bring me coffee in bed.
- Surprise me by folding and putting away all the laundry.
- Take out the trash.
- Ask me what's on my to-do list and take one thing off my plate.

- Give me a day off from everything and everyone (aka I want a hobby or spa day to myself).
- Wash my car.
- Cook me my favorite meal.

If you love deep connection:

- Plan a date night once a week where we unplug from our phones.
- Go on a twenty-minute walk with me after dinner.
- Take me to a new local restaurant.
- Ask me connecting questions.
- Arrange for us to have a special experience together (dancing, seeing a show, attending a wine and paint night, etc.).
- Watch a Marriage365 video with me.
- Put away your phone during family dinner.

If you love to be touched:

- Hold my hand when we're walking together or watching TV.
- Give me a back rub after a long day.
- Spontaneously kiss me so I know you desire me.
- Initiate sex.
- Pull me in close and cuddle with me in bed.
- Give me a long bear hug when I come home from work.

If you love gifts:

- Surprise me with my favorite beverage.
- Buy me something thoughtful, like a new book or T-shirt.
- Pick out something special that makes you think of me when you're at a store.

- Make a mental note when I mention something that I want and surprise me with it later.
- Plant my favorite flowers in the yard so I can look at them all the time.
- Look at my Amazon wish list and surprise me with something on it.
- Do an art project with our kids just for me.
- Surprise me with concert tickets.
- Draw or paint a card for me just because.

If you love experiences:

- Cook a new recipe with me.
- Run errands with me.
- Go for evening walks with me.
- Make a playlist with me.
- Plan a mini date for me (picnic, museum trip, comedy show).
- Book a class for us to take together (cooking, pottery, kayaking).

Think creatively. Your Love List doesn't have to match anyone else's expectations. For example, one couple shared that the husband loves when his wife joins him in the garage to tinker with his car—even if she just sits and reads a book. The act of being there speaks volumes to him. Prior to making his Love List, his wife had no idea! She never would have guessed that just sitting there with him, often in silence while the two of them focus on different things, meant so much to him. Another wife shared that her favorite act of love was when her husband planned a quiet coffee date at home one morning before the kids woke up. Simple, easy, powerful . . . and completely useless if you don't acknowledge it to yourself and share it with your spouse.

Once your lists are ready, exchange them and take turns reading them aloud. This is a chance to clarify any items that are vague, offer some modifications that make these requests a bit more realistic, and show gratitude for your spouse's thoughtfulness. During this part of the process, approach the conversation with curiosity and kindness. Avoid criticism or sarcasm, even if something surprises you—and especially if you think something on your spouse's list is stupid or meaningless. That might happen. If you don't care a thing for cars or sitting in silence with someone else, you might think sitting in the garage while your husband works is a silly way to spend time. But that's why that item isn't on *your* Love List. It's on theirs. Instead of shaming them for it, ask questions like "Why is this important to you?" or "How can I make this happen for you?"

Remember, this is about creating a road map for connection, not setting unrealistic expectations. The wife in a couple we worked with shared her Love List during a counseling session and had included "Plan a weekend getaway every six months." The husband initially felt overwhelmed by this request, explaining that they had a tight budget and little free time. But through the discussion, they modified the item to "Plan a fun date night out every other month." That compromise fulfilled the wife's desire for connection and effort while staying within their means. Over time, when life slows down and they have more expendable cash, they can work toward a getaway every now and then.

OUR LOVE LISTS

Meygan's top three items on her list include unloading the dishwasher, drawing her a bath with candles, and surprising her with a cappuccino from her favorite coffee shop. At first, Casey thought, *That's it? No grand romantic gestures?* But when he started doing these small things regularly, he saw how much they meant to her. Meygan is a big "acts of service" person. It wasn't specifically on her Love List, but one evening, Casey surprised her by taking over the entire bedtime routine for the kids. (Bonus tip: Knowing your partner's Love List will help spark other ideas for things you can do for them!) He bathed them, read their favorite stories, and tucked them in while she relaxed in the bath he'd drawn for her (which *was* on her list). Later, she told Casey it felt like a luxury hotel experience—and for the first time in a while, she felt truly appreciated. Casey's list includes encouraging him to go golfing on Friday afternoons. Meygan knows how hard it is for him to step away from work. To Casey, her support feels like a big hug, saying, "I see you, and I care about what makes you happy."

There are other benefits to Love Lists, beyond just making your spouse feel great. One of the most powerful effects is their tendency to de-escalate tension before we end up in conflict. During a particularly stressful month at work, Meygan noticed that Casey was quieter and more withdrawn than usual. Instead of guessing what might make him feel better, she revisited his Love List. That evening, she initiated a "walkie-talkie session"— our term for neighborhood strolls where we share about our day. It turned out that he was stressed about work. We were updating our app and had run into some roadblocks that slowed things down. Casey was disappointed and bummed that the process wasn't going as he'd hoped. That simple act helped him open up, and he felt an immediate sense of relief. Without it, Casey might have gone on sulking for days, and Meygan's frustration and resentment could have built up.

Another couple shared how their Love List saved them during a tense holiday season. The wife felt overwhelmed with hosting duties, while the husband was focused on buying gifts. Her Love List included "Help me prep for guests," and once he saw it, he jumped in to clean and set up, relieving her stress. In years past, this misalignment might have become a knock-down, drag-out brawl during what should be the most wonderful time of the year. Instead, their dynamic was peaceful, because each partner felt appreciated and cared for.

Meygan's Insight

Loving your spouse the way they want to be loved takes intentionality—yep, there's that word again. One simple thing that's helped me stay consistent is setting a phone reminder labeled "Love List." It keeps Casey's needs top of mind and saves me from those "Oh no, I forgot!" moments when I meant to do something meaningful but didn't follow through.

PRACTICAL TIPS

Here are a few additional tips to make the most of your Love Lists:

1. Revisit and update them regularly.

Your needs and preferences will change over time, so schedule a quarterly check-in to review and revise your lists together. One time Meygan updated her Love List to include going to a ballet together. After years of sharing what makes us feel loved, Casey had no idea she was interested in that. And she wasn't, until recently. Casey took her to a local production of *The Nutcracker*, even though he's certainly not a fan of ballet. But he loved watching Meygan light up while she relived her childhood ballerina days. And he was a huge fan of what happened later that night in our bed as a result of his thoughtfulness. Love Lists evolve, just like your marriage. Because we're constantly learning about ourselves too.

Love Lists

TWENTY WAYS TO SHOW ME LOVE

1. _____
2. _____
3. _____
4. _____
5. _____
6. _____
7. _____
8. _____
9. _____
10. _____
11. _____
12. _____
13. _____
14. _____
15. _____
16. _____
17. _____
18. _____
19. _____
20. _____

WORDS • ACTS • TOUCH • GIFTS • TIME

2. Start small.

You don't have to tackle the entire list at once. Choose one item each week to focus on, and let your efforts build over time. We want to acknowledge here that starting small might be most important if your marriage is in a bad spot. Maybe just speaking to each other seems hard, let alone doing an act of kindness for your partner. We get it—we've been there too. Try just one small thing, even just once a month, and grow from there as it feels right. Make him coffee without him asking. Write a nice sticky note and put it on her desk. Do something they've asked you to do a million times but you always forget. Try one tiny bid for connection and watch the ripple effects. Remember the flywheel effect? Just get that wheel spinning in the right direction.

3. Celebrate wins.

Acknowledge when your partner fulfills something on your list. Positive reinforcement encourages more of the same behavior. Repeat after us: "Thank you for . . . Thank you for . . . Thank you for . . ." That's all you have to do. Don't underestimate the power of acknowledging your spouse's efforts.

4. Be patient.

If your spouse struggles to articulate their needs or complete their list, offer gentle encouragement. Some people need more time to reflect on what makes them feel loved. Even harder, be patient if your spouse is slow to check off things on your Love List. Building habits takes time. Trying new things can be awkward and hard. Keep initiating Love List items and be patient as you both get used to this new part of your relationship.

5. Use Love Lists during tough times.

If you or your spouse is going through a rough patch, refer to the Love List as a guide. It can be a comforting tool to show love in ways that resonate deeply.

6. Make it fun.

One couple turned their Love List into a game. They both wrote down each item on slips of paper, put each person's slips in their own jar, and drew one slip at random every week. This added an element of surprise and kept things fresh. We have a whole chapter on fun coming up, so we have no shortage of ideas on how to mix things up. But just remember, marriage is supposed to be fun. Don't get too wrapped up in "doing it right" or potentially "failing" at this. You can't fail. If you're being curious and intentional, you're winning.

Ready to create your Love Lists? Remember, love is a choice—and Love Lists are a powerful tool to help you choose it every day. Start small, stay consistent, and watch your connection grow.

●━━━━━━━━━━━━●

CONNECTING QUESTIONS

1. What are some of your favorite memories of us, and how can we create more experiences like those?

2. Do you ever struggle with the ways I express my love? Why or why not?

3. How do you feel about the balance between giving and receiving love in our relationship?

4. What are your thoughts and feelings toward Love Lists and implementing this habit into our marriage?

5. What are some things that could get in the way of us making time and effort with our Love Lists (e.g., parenting, work schedules, finances, etc.)?

The 60-Second Blessing

Your words have power. Wield it wisely.

•————————————————•

When you were a kid, did you ever hear the phrase "Sticks and stones may break my bones, but words will never hurt me"? Yeah, that's BS. If you've ever been in an argument with your spouse, you know that one wrong sentence can turn an ordinary Tuesday into a battlefield. There's a proverb that says, "Death and life are in the power of the tongue, and those who love it . . . bear the consequences of their words." Words are incredibly powerful. They have the power to heal or to hurt. To quote Albus Dumbledore from the Harry Potter series, they're the "most inexhaustible source of magic."

Science backs this up too. Research from Drs. John and Julie Gottman, renowned marriage therapists, shows that for a relationship to thrive, couples must maintain a five-to-one ratio of positive to negative interactions. That means for every one argument, sarcastic comment, or complaint, you need five positive affirmations to counterbalance it. When we say that to couples in our intensives, the reaction is often "Yikes." When you think about your own relationship, can you honestly say that you have five times more positive reactions than negative ones? It's okay if you can't. We're about to help you with that. And you already know from the story of our marriage that we didn't live that way for years. Our record was probably something like ten negative interactions to one positive interaction. Maybe ten-to-none on our worst days.

Most couples don't even realize how much negativity seeps into their daily interactions. They're throwing out negative statements subconsciously, saying things like this:

- "It sure would be nice if you helped out."
- "Why do you always do that?"
- "I'm tired of having to ask over and over again for help."
- "I guess I'll do it myself."

These little jabs add up. But what if, instead, we intentionally filled our marriages with positive words? Even for just one minute a day? That's exactly what this chapter, the 60-Second Blessing, is all about. It's one minute of showering your spouse with positive words. And it might be the most powerful and important of the habits.

Some things in life are complicated. Taxes. Trying to fold a fitted sheet. Figuring out why your toddler is screaming when you just handed them the exact snack they asked for. But this is not one of those things. The 60-Second Blessing is exactly what it sounds like. For sixty seconds each, you and your spouse will take turns speaking words of love, appreciation, and admiration to each other.

CASEY'S COACHING CORNER

I tell couples that you plant either weed seeds or fruit trees with your words. Weed seeds kill your garden and make it much less desirable, but fruit trees grow, and you enjoy the delicious outcome.

No interruptions. No sarcasm. No "constructive criticism." Just pure, unadulterated encouragement and affirmation. Two minutes total. That's it. We like to do this standing, holding hands, and facing each other every morning. Bonus points if you do it in the KNOWN position.

Here's an example of what it might sound like:

Casey: "Meygan, I love your energy. The way you light up when you're passionate about something is magnetic. You're such a great mom, always making sure our kids feel seen and loved. You're also hilarious— I love how you sing musicals dramatically and dance in the kitchen. I really appreciate how you push me to be a better man and father. And I love your green eyes."

Meygan: "Casey, you are the most incredible dad. Watching you play with our kids makes me fall in love with you all over again. You make me feel safe, supported, and deeply loved. I love how you're always trying to make the world a better place. Thank you for teaching me how to be quick to forgive, and thank you for not holding grudges when I mess up. And, I mean, let's be real . . . I love your butt. It's sexy."

That's it. That's the whole exercise. And yet, this simple habit has the power to revolutionize your marriage.

Let us tell you about Jake and Lauren. If someone wrote a book about their marriage, it'd be called *The Couple Who Thought They Were Done*. When Jake and Lauren first came to us, they were on the brink of divorce. And we don't mean "Things are a little tense, but we're working through it." We mean they were sleeping in separate rooms, barely speaking, and feeling like there was nothing left to fight for.

They sat in our office, arms crossed, faces blank. You could feel the exhaustion in the air. Not the kind of exhaustion that comes from lack of sleep, but the kind that comes from years of struggling, fighting, and working on things just for nothing to ever actually work. It's that bone-tired feeling like you can't keep going and maybe it's time to throw in the towel.

Lauren spoke first. "I don't even know why we're here. We've tried everything, and nothing works." Jake sighed. "Yeah. We don't even like each other anymore." Oof. That's a heavy statement. But it's not uncommon. Heck, we've been there. Early in our marriage we had periods where we didn't like each other for months. When a couple has been through years of conflict, miscommunication, and resentment, it's easy to believe that the love is gone for good and the damage is permanent. Especially if you've already been to therapy and read some (other) books.

As we started digging into Jake and Lauren's story, something became painfully clear. Their marriage hadn't been destroyed by a single event—it had eroded over time. It wasn't one big betrayal or catastrophic mistake that landed them here. It was a million little moments of feeling unseen. Here's how Lauren saw things:

- She took care of the house.
- She handled the kids' schedules.
- She did all the little things that kept their life running.
- And she felt completely invisible, unappreciated for all the work she was doing.

Jake, on the other hand, felt like he couldn't win. This was his perspective:

- He worked hard to provide for their family, but nothing he did ever seemed to be enough.

- He stopped trying to connect with Lauren because he felt like she didn't care anymore.
- The resentment built up to the point where he emotionally checked out. Instead of spending intentional time together, going on dates, or even talking in the evening, he scrolled on his phone and watched TV. Every conversation was transactional, on autopilot, just going through the motions. It's a natural outcome of being hurt.

Again, what a terrible feeling. And no one was to blame. Or both were to blame. But it wasn't one person who tore it all down. It was one tiny slight after another that, over time, amounted to two people feeling like they hardly knew each other anymore. Sound familiar?

This is the slow drift that happens in so many marriages. Lauren and Jake didn't stop loving each other—but they stopped showing it. By the time they came to us, they were in a tough spot and reluctant to try much of anything we recommended. So we gave them only one assignment: Try the 60-Second Blessing for seven days. No therapy sessions. No deep emotional processing. Just two minutes a day.

Lauren rolled her eyes. "That's it? That's your advice?"

Yep.

Because here's the thing—words are powerful. And we knew that the words Lauren and Jake had been speaking over their marriage weren't life-giving. The only things that had grown from those words they'd spoken over the last few years were distance, doubt, and disconnection. So we challenged them to start planting some different seeds that might grow something new. They were skeptical. They didn't believe anything could fix their marriage at this point. But they agreed to try.

We warned them that the first couple of days would feel weird. And, oh boy, were we right. Lauren later told us she almost laughed out loud when Jake started his sixty seconds. He fumbled over his words. He felt and looked and sounded awkward. He struggled to find anything nice to say that didn't seem forced. Lauren's turn wasn't much better. She couldn't even make eye contact. But here's the important part: They did it anyway.

By the third day, something started to shift. After only two days, Lauren wasn't just going through the motions anymore. Instead of listing generic compliments, she said, "Jake, I know I haven't said this in a long time, but . . . I see how hard you work for us. I know I don't always act like it, but I really appreciate everything you do." Jake teared up. Remember, that was the exact wound he'd mentioned earlier. He spent years feeling unseen and unappreciated. Now his wife was speaking praise into that same place of vulnerability.

By the fifth day, something even more surprising happened. Jake and Lauren hugged. Now, that might not sound like a big deal, but for a couple that had been avoiding each other for months? It was huge. Lauren told us later, "It wasn't a big, dramatic moment. It just happened naturally. We had spent so many nights sleeping in separate beds, but that night? I actually wanted to be close to him." By the end of the week, they both agreed on one thing. "We don't actually hate each other. We just forgot how to love each other." That's the power of words. You start speaking life into your marriage, and connection follows.

Did the 60-Second Blessing fix everything overnight? Of course not. But it reminded them why they fell in love in the first place. It created safety—a place where they could slowly rebuild trust. It softened their hearts, making deeper conversations possible. And, ultimately, it saved their marriage.

WHY THIS WORKS

We know what you're thinking because we've heard the same question from hundreds of people. "Can two minutes a day really make that big of a difference?" Yes. And here's why.

1. It rewires your brain for positivity.

Science tells us that our brains have a negativity bias—we're wired to remember negative comments more than positive ones. And we're wired to notice negative things more than positive ones. So, that list of all those things your spouse has done "wrong" that you've been internally tallying for years? It's not *entirely* your fault. Your brain likes to do that. It's easier than remembering and noticing the "right" things. If you've ever had someone criticize you once, and it stuck with you for years, that's negativity bias at work.

The 60-Second Blessing helps retrain your brain to notice the good in your spouse. When you're actively looking for things to affirm, your focus shifts from what's wrong to what's right. For those of you whose marriage is in a dark place, know this: The good in them *is* there. It was there when you were dating, and it's still there. You might just have to think a little harder to recognize it.

2. It builds emotional safety.

One of the biggest reasons couples drift apart isn't a lack of love. It's a lack of emotional safety. When you feel criticized, unappreciated, or unseen, you start to shut down. The 60-Second Blessing counteracts that by making sure each partner feels valued, loved, and safe.

A study in the *Journal of Personality and Social Psychology* found that couples who regularly express appreciation for each other have higher relationship satisfaction and report feeling more secure and connected. You guys are a team. And it's impossible to feel connected with your teammate if you don't feel safe. Emotional safety is what allows us to open up about hard things and allows our partner to help us or know us deeper. And it becomes a lifeline when you are grieving a miscarriage, working through conflict with extended family, having financial struggles, caring for aging parents, or navigating parenting trials. You create that space for the big, hard things with these small, daily affirmations.

3. It strengthens trust and repairs damage.

Trust isn't built in one climactic moment. It's built or lost in tiny, everyday interactions. Even couples who have broken trust because of one big, glaring mistake (whether through betrayal, dishonesty, or emotional neglect) can use consistent positive affirmations to rebuild their connection. If you're like Jake and Lauren and can't point to a single moment when things turned, you can use this simple tool to rebuild trust day after day. And it probably won't even take as long as you think.

You should feel incredibly powerful knowing that you can help heal some of the deepest wounds your partner carries—whether you caused them or not. They likely have scars from childhood, past relationships, and beyond that, and you can help heal them. You have influence that no one else has. Because, regardless of the state of your relationship, words from you still hold more weight than words from almost anyone else in their life. They land differently. Use them for good.

HOW IT WORKS

For some couples, the 60-Second Blessing will feel awkward at first. That's okay. Start where you are. You just need two minutes of courage to get going.

Step 1: Write it down first if you need to.

If coming up with words on the spot feels overwhelming, write down five to ten things you love about your spouse before you begin. Then, just read them out loud. Eventually the words will come naturally and you won't need so much prep. But here are some ideas if you're just starting out:

- Compliment a physical trait.
- Appreciate a role they play in their family, work, or community.

- Point out a unique trait of theirs that makes them one of a kind.
- Reflect back a strength of theirs.
- Comment on how they make you feel.
- Tell them what you enjoy about them.
- Name something positive about their character, personality, appearance, parenting, work ethic, effort, or accomplishments.

There are, of course, so many more. But this will get you started. Again, over time, you won't need these guidelines. This will come much easier the more you do it.

Step 2: Do it every day for seven days. (And hopefully longer.)

Full disclosure: The two of us no longer do the 60-Second Blessing every single day. We don't have to. Our marriage is in a much better place, so if we skip a couple of days of blessings, it's no big deal. But if you're just starting out, and especially if you're in crisis, we guarantee you'll notice a difference if you try doing this every day for one week. That's just fourteen minutes total. On our hardest days, or when life gets busy and we start feeling disconnected, we always make sure the 60-Second Blessing happens. We even put it on the calendar. It's also on both of our Love Lists, so when either of us is down or there's tension, it's a way for us to turn things around.

Step 3: Keep it up. (Even on hard days.)

Here are some of the most important times to practice the 60-Second Blessing:

- After a fight (yes, even when you don't feel like it)
- Before bed or in the morning to start the day
- In the evening to end the day on a positive note

- In front of your kids, so they can see healthy, loving communication (even if it means keeping the physical trait stuff G-rated)
- During date night or connection time

Bonus: Use this with your kids.

The world constantly bombards our kids with messages that they aren't enough. They hear things like this:

- "You're not smart enough."
- "You're not talented enough."
- "You're not successful enough."

But as their parents, we have the power to counteract all that. We've made the 60-Second Blessing a regular practice in our family. We do it with our kids, and sometimes we even ask them to do it with each other. (They grumble at first, but they secretly love it.)

A good place to try this is at the dinner table. Take turns going around and affirming one family member. Watch how it shifts the atmosphere in your home.

Here are a few more quick tips:

- If you can't be together physically because one of you is out of town, you can always call, text, or email your 60-Second Blessing. (We've seen this exercise be exceptionally powerful for military couples.) Doing this practice, even just by email, can help you stay connected over the distance and get you through the hardest times.

- If doing a daily 60-Second Blessing feels like too much, you can start with just a few times a week. Or even just once. Something is always better than nothing. We're huge fans of the seven-day challenge, but like all the habits, you can adapt this one however you need to. Just begin building momentum. Get the flywheel going. Start building the habit, no matter what it takes.

- Try not to repeat too many compliments. Obviously it does get hard to keep coming up with new material every single day over many months, but get creative. Some of the best blessings are super specific. You can compliment your spouse on something they did yesterday or an event from years ago. Don't keep saying, "I love how kind you are" day after day. Specificity is the antidote to repetition. Men, if you love complimenting your wife's breasts but don't want to say, "You have great boobs" every day, try "Your boobs looked incredible in that tank top yesterday." Remember, the point of the 60-Second Blessing is to rewire you for positivity. Start actively looking for things you can compliment later.

MEYGAN'S INSIGHT

When you're running low on fresh things to say, look for the little things—something your spouse did or said in the last few days that caught your attention. You'd be surprised how meaningful it is when someone notices the "small stuff," like unloading the dishwasher or making the bed, and actually says thank you. I also like to rewind and pull from our dating years—those early butterflies, the way Casey's smile lit up the room (and still does). Recalling those fun, feel-good memories makes the blessing even more powerful.

Do not underestimate this habit. Words shape worlds. And when those words are intentional, kind, and consistent, they can begin to repair the cracks you didn't even realize had formed—in yourself and in your marriage. This is how a relationship gets rewired: not in grand romantic gestures or Instagram-worthy vacations, but in everyday moments where you choose to speak life. Sixty seconds a day becomes a thread that weaves you back together.

CONNECTING QUESTIONS

1. Did you see your parents speak positive and kind words or critical and hurtful words to each other?

2. Can you remember a time when something I said really encouraged you? What was it?

3. Are there any words or phrases I say that make you feel especially valued?

4. When you're having a hard day, what's the best thing I can say to lift you up?

5. Would you be willing to commit to the 60-Second Blessing for seven days and why?

Connection Time

It's not that serious. Just have some fun.

No matter the state of your marriage, here's something we're willing to bet is absolutely true: When you and your spouse were dating, you had fun. You wouldn't have gotten married if you didn't, right? Maybe you shared a hobby, maybe you laughed until your stomach hurt, maybe you went on spontaneous adventures, maybe your idea of fun was just playing a card game on a cozy night in. But you did have fun, and that's why you kept dating. If date numbers one and two were boring, there wouldn't have been dates three, four, or five—let alone a wedding. But now, you might feel like your marriage is all responsibilities, schedules, and stress. Maybe the fun you once had seems like a distant memory.

At the beginning of this book, we told you that we are not, nor have we ever claimed to be, all-knowing relationship gurus. There's a lot we don't know. But fun? Fun, we *know*. At many of our lowest points, fun has been the glue that held us together. Even when we've felt like we had nothing else, we had fun.

In 2008, within five years of getting married, we lost everything. We were broke and living with Meygan's mom. So we bought a ten-dollar blue plastic pool from a local drugstore. We couldn't fit it inside our tiny Honda Civic, and we hadn't brought anything to tie it to the top of the car, so we drove all the way home with one arm each out of a window, holding the pool in place. We looked at each other that whole ride home, our car basically crawling down the road to ensure the pool wouldn't fly away, and laughed until we cried. We didn't have money, a home, or a plan. We barely even had jobs. But we had fun. When we got home, we filled up that tiny pool in the backyard with a hose, and it became our temporary escape. We crammed ourselves and our nine-month-old daughter into it, splashing around and laughing because it was all we had. During one of the hardest seasons of our life, fun single-handedly kept us going.

Marriage is often sold as "hard work." You hear about sacrifice, embracing the mundane, handling conflict, and managing in-laws. But what doesn't get talked about enough is that marriage also brings companionship, laughter, adventure, and *fun*. Fun is what makes the hard times bearable, the routine moments enjoyable, and the connection between you and your spouse strong. Many of the couples who come to us don't really need more coaching or tools for communication—they just need to have more fun. That's why one of the questions we always ask couples in a coaching session is "When was the last time you two had fun together?" A common response is "I can't remember."

Unfortunately, fun hasn't been studied nearly as much as other topics in marriage, like conflict, communication, or connection. But the research that has been done shows that fun is pretty dang important. It's often couched in jargony conclusions like "Couples who engage in shared leisure activities and maintain a playful dynamic experience stronger emotional connections and higher marital satisfaction. For instance, studies have found that couples participating in joint leisure activities report more stable and satisfying marriages." *Nerd alert!* A study published in *The Canadian Journal of Human Sexuality* even suggests that couples who joke about their sex lives are more likely to enjoy greater satisfaction in their sexual experiences. So go ahead, take yourselves a little less seriously.

Many marriage books—including this one, to some degree—focus on getting rid of bad marriage habits or patterns. They tell you "Stop doing this" or "Don't do that." But working on your marriage can't be just about cutting out the bad stuff. It puts too bright a spotlight on those hard things. That's why, when a dietitian is helping someone lose weight, they will often first address adding good things into the person's diet before they focus on cutting out the unhealthy stuff. It creates a more positive and abundant mindset. No one likes to feel restricted or chastised.

The same is true with marriage. We give you full permission to focus on adding in the good, fun, frivolous, and joyful—at least for a while. Maybe you don't need more talk therapy about active listening; you just need a little more mini golf. Maybe instead of having yet another conversation about your budget, you should play Monopoly or go skinny-dipping in the lake. Nothing builds connection like having fun.

CASEY'S COACHING CORNER

Listen, there may be legitimate hurts that need to be dealt with, but playfulness can also communicate that we are still committed to a "we." This is a moment that can break the ice in many relationships and help spouses reassure each other that there's still a relationship to work on. I've talked to many husbands, in particular, who are so wound up with work that they've forgotten how to get in touch with their fun self. Fun can spark the romance you are looking for.

If fun is so much fun . . . why do most couples lose it at some point? It's never on purpose, we know that much. Usually, the loss doesn't come down to a specific moment but a series of small decisions that, over time, add up to way more seriousness and way less fun. Let's look at what those could be.

WHAT'S GETTING IN THE WAY OF FUN?

1. You have unresolved conflict.

It's nearly impossible to have fun with someone you're still mad at. When hurts aren't healed, when apologies aren't made, when trust isn't rebuilt, resentment takes root. And resentful couples are not laughing couples. We're going to get into apologies and forgiveness in later chapters. But for now, just know that if you are deep in conflict, having fun will naturally be harder for you.

2. You're struggling with emotional laziness.

As things become more familiar, we often unintentionally become lazier about them. In marriage, this can look like putting in less effort, stopping the deep conversations, and just coexisting. Autopilot is not a fun setting for marriage. We've all been there. But remember the intentionality piece of the marriage mindset. Just because you're having fun on purpose doesn't make it any less fun.

3. Your schedules are busy.

If your schedule is packed with work, kids, chores, and obligations, you may not have space left for fun. If every ounce of energy is spent on others, you'll collapse into bed exhausted, wondering why you don't feel connected to your spouse anymore. This is often the first way people start losing out on fun. It seems pretty benign. You have kids and life gets full. It's normal, not harmful. But over time, the life administration busyness blocks out all the fun. In our work-hard culture that prioritizes productivity over almost everything, fun gets knocked down the list of activities. We cannot stress enough: Fun is important. It's productive, even. Anything that brings you closer to your spouse should be important to you.

4. You've lost the ability to play.

Some people just take themselves too seriously. As kids, we played and explored the world. As adults, we get weighed down by responsibilities, and somewhere along the way, we stop playing. Fun starts feeling immature or unimportant. But it's not. It's essential.

5. You need to overcome insecurities.

Fun requires a level of comfort and confidence, the kind that allows you to be goofy, silly, and playful. But if you've got insecurities, you may struggle to relax and enjoy yourself. This is especially true for couples who are really hurting. If your spouse has hurt your feelings, it's understandable that you'd find it hard to be vulnerable and let down your guard. Take baby steps. In the following pages, we've included a whole list of ideas for adding some fun into your marriage. If you're afraid to do something intimate (like a naked dinner), just try going on a bike ride or watching a show together. This is about fun. If you pick something that feels not fun for you, well . . . you're doing it wrong.

HOW TO REINTRODUCE FUN IN YOUR MARRIAGE

1. Identify the barrier.

Before you can add fun back into your relationship, you have to address what's blocking it. Is it unresolved conflict? Start with sincere apologies, forgiveness, and rebuilding trust. (We'll get into those in a later chapter.) Emotional laziness? Stop taking your spouse for granted and start prioritizing quality time during your Weekly Marriage Business Meeting. A packed schedule? Start saying no to outside obligations and yes to your relationship.

2. Make a fun list.

Waiting until the last minute to figure out how to have fun is like waiting until five thirty in the evening to decide what's for dinner. It leads to frustration and wasted opportunities. Instead, make a list of fun activities in advance. Here are some of our favorites:

- Relive your first date.
- Take dance lessons.
- Have a naked dinner (seriously, just try it!). Though we do recommend cooking fully clothed.
- Look through old pictures and ticket stubs from your dating days.
- Play a card game at a coffee shop. We love rummy and Yahtzee.
- Take a bike ride through town.
- Plan a twenty-dollar date-night challenge. Go out on a date and don't spend more than twenty dollars. It's harder than you think and forces you to get creative.
- Build a fort in the living room (bonus points if you have sex in it).
- Have a Nerf gun fight in the house.
- Play cornhole, Ping-Pong, or some other game activity.
- Do crossword puzzles or sudoku.
- Take a walk in nature.
- Rent a boat for the day.

3. Put fun on the calendar.

If you think you're too busy for fun . . . well, first of all you're wrong. Second, you need to schedule it. It might feel weird at first, but prioritizing fun ensures that it actually happens. Like sex, we promise putting it on the calendar won't make it any less enjoyable. If possible, take turns planning activities so both spouses get a chance to contribute. Do this during your WMBM.

CASEY'S COACHING CORNER

As someone who's spontaneous and motivated by fun, I found the idea of scheduling fun a challenge at first. But I had to realize two things: (1) that I married a type A, organized person who appreciates schedules, and (2) that leaving this connection time up to chance makes it rarely happen. Fail to plan, plan to fail, right? Once we had the scheduled fun, I didn't mind that it had been on the calendar. Fun was the goal, and we were having it.

---

4. Make sex fun again.

Some couples take sex too seriously—like it's a performance instead of an experience. The bedroom should be a place of play, laughter, and connection. If an awkward moment happens, laugh about it. We'll get into this more in the sex chapter. Find ways to keep intimacy lighthearted and enjoyable.

5. Focus on gratitude.

Joyful people are grateful people. Instead of focusing on what your marriage lacks, focus on what it has. The more you appreciate what you have, the easier it is to find joy in the everyday moments. Think about the daily things that are easy to take for granted: your house, health, food in your pantry, a book you're enjoying. A simple way to cultivate gratitude is by writing down five things you're grateful for each day. Over time, this habit shifts your perspective and helps you recognize the small but meaningful blessings in your life and marriage. This is also a fun exercise to do as a couple or family.

What if my spouse isn't fun?

We hear this a lot: "I'm a fun person, but my spouse isn't." Here's the reality—if your spouse was fun when you were dating, they can be fun again. They just need to be reminded how, and you might need to help them. At first, you might be the one scheduling and prioritizing fun. But we also know that there are just some people in the world who are naturally more serious. Some people are quite reserved, and that's completely fine. If your spouse wasn't especially fun even when you were dating, then fun wasn't one of your nonnegotiables, and there were other qualities that made you fall in love with them. Focus on those strengths instead. You can still gently encourage more fun in your relationship, especially if it's important to you and your spouse knows that and cares. But if they've always been this way, expecting them to change may be unfair. Everyone has different values, and if fun isn't one of theirs, that's okay. Focus on what you do enjoy and appreciate.

DATE NIGHT DONE RIGHT

In 2023 we polled our Instagram followers, and 8,200 people responded. We asked, "If you could improve one thing about your date nights, what would it be?" Two-thirds of them (66 percent) answered "more consistency." That answer won over "more creative/fun ideas," "less distractions," and "better communication." You know by now what our solution is: Schedule it.

Think back to before you were married. How did you spend your time together? You went on date nights! Day dates! Breakfast dates! Movie dates! Adventurous dates! When you think about it, everything was kind of a date back then. You spent quality and quantity time together. You didn't do chores or pay bills together or scroll through your phone for hours. You made time in your schedule to hang out, have fun, talk, and probably make out. You hardly had to intentionally remember to plan a date night, because your entire life consisted of dating. Then, along the way, you got married and slowly stopped dating your spouse.

That ends now. For a successful date night, there are only three rules you need to follow. Don't get freaked out by the word *rules*. Remember, we're your fun czars! These rules, or suggestions, are to protect your time together so you don't end up fighting or disconnecting. The point is to make your dates even better.

1. Don't talk about work.

If you had a terrible day at the office and you just need to vent and let it all out before you can enjoy your time together, we get it. Do what we call the five-minute rule. You get five minutes to vent about your boss or that annoying customer, but then be done with it. Move on and don't allow it to consume your entire evening. If you and your spouse work together like we do, this is a really, really hard goal to follow. You most likely will break from time to time. Just do your best and make sure you have separate meetings that are all about work.

2. Don't talk about money or finances.

For most people, money talks are not a turn-on. Don't spend your precious connection time talking about the budget or an upcoming expense or your savings goals. The best time to talk about money is during your Weekly Marriage Business Meeting.

3. Don't talk about the kids.

We get it. They're cute and expensive and amazing. But this is your date night, not theirs. Everything else is probably about them. Let this be about you. The second most common life stage for people to divorce is when they become empty nesters (the first is years four through ten). They let their marriage become all about the kids and never invested in their relationship. Let's prevent that by making sure you actually connect during that time you've set apart for each other.

Oftentimes, if couples haven't connected throughout their week about the logistics of life—who's taking the kids to school and what you need to buy for your mom's upcoming birthday and the new tires you're putting on the car—they'll be tempted to bring up those things during their date night. This is why committing to the Weekly Marriage Business Meeting is so important. Your date night is only about laughing, making new memories, connecting emotionally, and having intimate conversations—the transformational stuff. The WMBM is where you get to talk about all the adulting and unsexy parts of life, the transactional conversations.

Here's another little bonus tip: A lot of couples schedule sex right after their weekly date night. It makes sense. Hopefully that's a time when you're feeling connected and emotionally safe. Sex could be a natural outcome of time together. But there are certain spouses who get annoyed that sex is expected that night. It might take away from the authenticity of the rest of the date or make them anxious anticipating the evening. There isn't a right or a wrong way to do it, but if you're doing date night just to have sex, that's not a good mindset. You should be doing date night because you love and care for your partner and you want to make your marriage a priority. For some, it might make sense to separate sex from your date night so this priority is clear to your spouse.

HOW TO DREAM WITH YOUR SPOUSE

We want to end this chapter with a simple and fun exercise that will help you and your spouse connect emotionally: dreaming about your future. Like date night, this is another way to leave the boring logistics of life behind for a minute and remember who you are and what you want. It also builds trust, security, and safety in your relationship. When you have a conversation about your hopes and dreams for your future, it communicates, "I love you, I see us living a long and happy life together, and I care about what you want and who you're becoming."

Here's how this works. Set aside ten to twenty minutes, depending on how chatty you both are, to walk through these three questions.

1. What is one thing you want to do in the future together as a couple?

It may be traveling to a new country or starting a new hobby together. Or maybe it's just getting the dog you've always wanted. For us, we talk about all the things we want to do as grandparents once our kids are grown and married. For a while, "write a book on marriage" was on our dream list. Now we're doing just that. Here's a word of caution: Your spouse may say something that surprises you. Don't freak out or judge their dreams. It will destroy any kind of opportunity for emotional connection. Also remember that some people need time to think and process. If your partner can't come up with an answer right away, it's okay. Don't badger them. Share your dreams and then check in with them in the next day or two.

2. What's one thing you want to do on your own at some point in the next twenty years?

This gives each of you an opportunity to think about the dreams that are uniquely yours. Maybe your spouse had these dreams before they met you, and getting back in touch with those dreams would bring them a lot of joy. For example, one of the things Casey mentioned to Meygan when we did this exercise was that he wants to go back to school and get his master's degree. Meygan didn't share that excitement for going back to school after being in it for eighteen years, but she loved knowing and supporting that in Casey. What's cool about this question is that you get to learn more about your spouse *and* understand how you can better support them.

3. What are some things we need to implement, change, or plan for so these dreams can become a reality?

This is where things get practical. Talking about goals and dreams is exciting, but most people want to make sure their future together actually happens. We encourage you to make a to-do list and create an action plan. You may be in a season of life where there isn't much you can do to make these dreams happen yet, and that's okay. The fact that you're talking about them is a step in the right direction. You could also create a dream or vision board. Choose visuals that represent your goals, like pictures of a vacation spot, a home you dream of, or a quote that keeps you motivated.

MEYGAN'S INSIGHT

Remember, you're in the fun chapter, and this is supposed to be a fun exercise. You're talking, laughing, learning, and hopefully connecting on a deeper level. Stay away from judgment and minimizing statements like "Why would you ever want to do that?" I'm guilty of this, big-time. Say it with me now: Be supportive. Your spouse's dreams don't have to be your dreams. But because they're the dreams of the person you love, you should at least care, listen thoughtfully, and help them come to fruition.

When our marriage was on the brink of falling apart, the only thing we had in common was fun. We weren't great with money, communication, or boundaries. But we could still laugh together. We played board games, joked around, and found moments to enjoy each other—even in our mess. That thread of fun held us together long enough to work on the other parts of our marriage. If you're in a tough season too, fun might feel impossible. But we promise, finding joy in the little things will help pull you through. Fun is the heartbeat of a lasting, connected, thriving marriage.

CONNECTING QUESTIONS

1. What's the most memorable date we've been on? What made it so memorable?

2. What are some things that have gotten in the way of us spending quality time together?

3. What are your thoughts about the three date-night rules (no talking about work, the kids, or money)?

4. What are your thoughts about sex after (or during) date night?

5. What are some things you enjoy doing during date night (e.g., talking, laughing, going on an adventure, experiencing physical touch, etc.)?

6. Other than date nights, is there any other way you like to connect emotionally and have fun together?

Leverage Your Differences

Discover your hidden superpowers.

——●————————————●——

Every year in America, hundreds of thousands of couples check the "irreconcilable differences" box on their divorce papers. A survey by the Institute for Divorce Financial Analysts found that 43 percent of people reported they were getting divorced because of "basic incompatibility." It means that a couple has fundamental disagreements or issues they cannot solve. It's safe to say that differences are often seen not only as a problem in marriage but also a reason to quit.

If you haven't been able to tell so far, we—Casey and Meygan—are pretty dang different from each other. When we were dating, these differences didn't seem to get in the way. When you're just courting your partner, you don't have to really work together as a team yet. It's easier to have respect for your differences when they haven't started to become a pain in your butt. You also focus more on the positives because you've got your love goggles on. Most of what you see are the traits you have in common.

Then you become an official team. The novelty wears off, and you are trying to move as one through life with budgets, meal

plans, parenting, scheduling. In dating, differences can feel exciting. But in marriage, they feel risky—especially when stress or
decision fatigue hits. So instead of leaning in, we try to control or
correct. We want comfort, not curiosity. We assume our partner
should think, feel, and respond like we do, and when they don't,
we feel misunderstood, even scared. One or both partners begin
to wonder, *How do I get my spouse to think like I do?* That would
make life a whole lot easier, right? When we get stuck in this
mindset, it can become messy for our relationships.

Here's how it usually goes:

1. *You start hyper-focusing on the differences.* Instead of
   seeing your partner's quirks and preferences as being
   complementary, you see them as obstacles.

2. *You try to "fix" your spouse.* Through nagging, passive-
   aggressiveness, or outright arguing, you attempt to
   mold them into a version of yourself.

3. *Frustration builds.* The more your efforts fail, the
   more resentment sets in.

4. *You withdraw.* Instead of leaning in and working together, you start pulling away.

5. *You begin to believe the biggest lie: Maybe I married the
   wrong person.*

At first, your tactics are subtle. A passive-aggressive comment
here, a well-placed sigh there. Then it escalates to full-blown manipulation. Like the time Casey tried to trick Meygan into liking
cooking by gifting her cookbooks, suggesting she spend more time
with our friend who loves to cook, and making comments like "It'd
be so fun to cook together!" It was Casey's way of trying to change
her instead of appreciating that she brings other strengths to our
marriage. It wasn't subtle or helpful, and most of all, it really hurt.

If you've engaged in any of this subtle manipulation to change your partner or sway them to your ways, don't worry. We all have. It's not great, but it's normal human behavior. Don't beat yourself up. And if your spouse has done it to you, don't beat them up either.

Here's the thing: Your differences aren't the problem. It's how we handle differences that makes or breaks a marriage. Say it with us now: Differences are *not* bad. Your differences aren't obstacles—they're your superpowers . . . if you stop trying to "fix" each other.

Too often, the conversation around marital differences involves language like "managing" the differences or "navigating" them. We'll address conflict in the next chapter, because no relationship is immune to it. But differences are different. They are not meant to be managed. They're meant to be celebrated and strengthened.

At one of our marriage retreats, a man stood up and shared about the differences in his relationship. He told us that he wasn't known as a warm, affectionate person, but his wife was. Over the years she'd offered their children and him so much comfort and kindness when they needed it—something he knew he wasn't great at. His spouse then shared that she was a people pleaser, but his directness and sturdiness had given her so much confidence over the years. She felt protected and empowered. Do you think these differences also caused conflict at points? Of course they did. But this couple had chosen to see them in a positive light.

We're realists here. There will be *plenty* of things about your spouse that will *always* bug you. What we want to accomplish is giving you some tools to help you see those differences as, at best, positives that strengthen your marriage and, at worst, things that don't cause such a rift that you head down the path to divorce.

COMMON DIFFERENCES THAT CAUSE CONFLICT

Before we can start appreciating our differences, we have to understand them. Sometimes, even that is enough to make progress. We hear couples say all the time, "We're so different," but they don't really define how or what that means. So, we're going to walk through some of the most common, tangible differences we see and how they've affected us and people we work with.

Introvert vs. Extrovert

One person thrives in social settings, while the other needs solitude to recharge. Both of us are extroverts, so okay, we're starting with the one we actually do have in common. We both love parties and being out with friends. But this is one of the most common differences we see in couples we work with. Often when an extrovert marries an introvert, the extrovert feels weighed down or like they're losing out on experiences because the introvert would rather be at home. Or the introvert might feel like their needs aren't being respected or met because they're tired all the time from going with their partner to all their social events.

Planner vs. Go with the Flow

The planner loves structure, while the go-with-the-flow partner craves spontaneity. Can you guess which one each of us is? Yep, maybe Meygan's strongest trait out of all these is her penchant for planning. Casey, of course, is the easygoing one who flows. When these two types marry each other, the planner can feel stressed and out of control when the more spontaneous person pulls a fast one. On the other hand, the easygoing partner may feel suffocated by a rigorous calendar. This is one of our starkest differences and something we've had to work hard on.

On Time vs. Late

Here's another big Casey and Meygan difference: One of us believes that being on time actually means you're late, and the other couldn't care less. (We'll let you guess who's who.) This often corresponds with the preceding difference. Planners like to be on time, and go-with-the-flow folks don't mind being a bit late. With Casey's ADHD, this is a big struggle for us. His lateness is not a sign of disrespect, like Meygan assumed at the beginning, but a result of his distractibility.

Early Bird vs. Night Owl

This one is obvious. One wants to wake up at sunrise, and the other comes alive after dark. This isn't as values driven as some of the other differences, but it can really mess up your schedules and connection time. If one person is always up late and the other up early, it's easy to get in a rhythm where you never see each other. It's also harder to assign responsibilities evenly when you have kids and work schedules to balance.

Spender vs. Saver

The spender sees money as freedom, while the other sees it as security. Financial issues are one of the most common reasons couples get divorced. One of the biggest "irreconcilable differences." Money is a representation of our values, which makes it about much more than just wealth. What we do with our money reflects the things we prioritize and our beliefs. There's more here to consider about money, but the best way to start appreciating your financial differences is to simply consider which you are: a spender or a saver. And remember that the world needs both savers and spenders.

MEYGAN'S INSIGHT

One tip that's been a game changer for us as a spender-and-saver couple is what we call a "blow fund." Every month, we each get a set amount of money to spend however we want—no questions, no guilt, no explanations needed. It gives the spender freedom and helps the saver loosen up and enjoy spending a little too. This simple habit has brought peace to both our budget and our marriage. Some months it's $75, other months it's $300—the amount flexes based on our income and what's happening that month.

Fighter vs. Flighter

The fighter wants to tackle conflict head-on, while the flighter avoids it at all costs. We find that this one is often biological. It's about how your body and brain respond during conflict. Some people have the instinct to run and avoid. And some dive in head-long, ready to go at it for as long as they need to. Casey is highly triggered by conflict. It pushes on his abandonment wound. For Meygan, the avoidance makes her nervous. She'd way rather tackle it head-on. Because Casey's nervous system can't tell the difference between Meygan saying, "Hey, we need to talk" and being chased by a bear, this causes some problems. Of all the differences we've discussed, this is one of the deepest for every relationship. Marriages with a fighter and a flighter can be amazing (look at us!), but you'll have to do some real work to understand this instinct in your spouse. More on that later.

Thinker vs. Feeler

Thinkers and feelers are wired totally differently. A thinker tends to approach problems with logic first: "What's the solution? What makes sense? Let's fix it and move on." Feelers, on the other hand, want to sit in the emotion for a minute. They're asking, "How is this affecting us? Do you see how I'm feeling?" They don't *think* about the problem as much as they *feel* the problem. Neither is wrong—but if you're a thinker married to a feeler, it can look like your spouse is overreacting. And if you're a feeler married to a thinker, it can feel like your spouse is cold or checked out. In many couples, the men are the thinkers and the women are the feelers, though in our case, Casey is the feeler and Meygan is the thinker.

Think about your own relationship. What are some other areas where you and your spouse are regularly at odds? We've seen couples have knock-down, drag-out fights over all kinds of differences: the appropriate amount of air-conditioning, whether the blinds should be up or down, and what time they should eat dinner. Here are a few areas you might consider in your relationship:

- *Family boundaries:* One spouse doesn't appreciate how involved the other spouse's family is in their life or marriage.
- *Politics:* We have seen some couples really go at it over this. Especially during election years, stark political differences can make things tense in the home.
- *Faith and spirituality:* This is a big one because our faith often informs so much else about our lives. Culturally, we're seeing a rise in couples who share the same faith when they get married, but over time, one changes their beliefs. Obviously, this has ripple effects in your marriage.
- *Parenting:* It's common to have one parent who is stricter and another who is the "fun" one. Everything from discipline to school decisions to schedules and routine can be affected by the differences in the parents.
- *Lifestyle:* Maybe one spouse is into eating clean foods, exercising, and meditating, while the other is less so. Perhaps the other prefers more leisure activities and considers a strict eating or workout routine too restrictive.
- *Music:* This is one most of you likely won't have to consider, but we wanted to add it as an example of how anything can manifest as a difference in your marriage that you might have to handle. In the past, Meygan notoriously did not listen to music. She pre-

fers the house to be quiet and to have a more Zen-like feel. Casey loves music. It has something to do with his ADHD. We (somewhat embarrassingly) had to work hard to understand this difference in each other.

How have these differences—and others—shown up in your relationship? Try not to judge whether they're deep or superficial. Sometimes people don't work on a tension point because they feel like it shouldn't bother them. We want you to know, there are no "shouldn'ts" here. If a difference is causing a rift in your marriage, it's worth addressing.

HOW TO APPRECIATE YOUR DIFFERENCES

Now that you've identified some ways you and your spouse are different, let's discuss what to do about it.

1. Recognize that differences are normal.

Hopefully, you've already done some of this. Since we busted the myth early on that marriage is a fairy tale, ideally you've come to terms with this idea. Differences are normal and okay. They will not destroy you. Healthy marriages are made up of secure and aware individuals. Try your best to own how you are different and don't deny or ignore it. There is a lot of relief and peace in that. Conflicting ideas and personalities are not a sign that your marriage is ending. It's just another Tuesday.

CASEY'S COACHING CORNER

Personality tests help create windows of understanding and even language around each other's strong points. My favorite go-to assessments are CliftonStrengths (formerly known as StrengthsFinder), 16Personalities, Myers-Briggs Type Indicator, and the Enneagram. Choose one and do a couple's night where you share your results. Print them, swap, and read each other's. Then each of you share one thing that resonated deeply, one thing that surprised you, and one small change you'll make after learning this.

2. Rate the importance of each issue.

This is where things get interesting. Not every difference is worth a battle. For each of the common differences we listed above, or for the ones you've decided on for your own marriage, we want you to ask yourself, *On a scale of one to ten, how important is this to me?* Then, share your answers with your spouse. A one means it barely matters, and a ten means it's the most important thing in the world to you.

Here's an example. When we were first figuring out how to deal with our wildly different approaches to punctuality, we did this ranking exercise. Casey rated anything to do with timeliness a four, while Meygan ranked it a ten. Everything about Meygan, from her innate personality to the way she was raised, inclines her to be early. It is extremely important. Her whole family is this way. Being late is a sign of disrespect and sets off her anxiety. Since Casey was a chronically late person, it regularly caused big fights that seemed disproportionate to the issue. Until we did this exercise.

The first benefit of this tool is that it simply brings awareness to how important the area of difference is to each of you—which might help one or both of you know when to let it go. Sometimes right smack in the middle of a debate about a topic, it's a good idea to stop and ask, "How important is this to you?" Just that simple break can help you move forward. It gives you a perspective on how your partner is thinking, feeling, and valuing this topic.

We once had a couple come to us for what they considered an "unsolvable problem." The wife couldn't understand why her husband never wanted to be involved with her extended family. She felt unsupported and unloved by him in this way. We had them rate this topic and, unsurprisingly, she ranked it a ten, and he ranked it a two. "A two!" she cried. He felt a little embarrassed by this, and we applauded his honesty. He hadn't been raised in a tight-knit family, and though he loved his wife deeply, he really did not care about a relationship with her extended family, as hard as that was for her to understand.

The goal here is to bring awareness of how important this is to each of you. When one of you ranks an issue high, and the other ranks it low, we suggest that the spouse with the lower number lean in, get curious, and try to understand why it's so important to your partner. Then, if possible, we encourage you to adjust to your spouse as an act of love. It's important to them, and because you care about them, try to make an effort.

For issues that you both rank low, that's great news. Maybe you've been making mountains out of molehills, and you both need to Let. It. Go. For the sake of your marriage and your peace.

But what happens when you both rate something very high? What we want more than anything, in this scenario, is to know that we are not crazy and that our spouse sees our perspective. You don't have to agree with them to validate them. For example, the two of us have very different parenting styles and have even said, "I don't fully agree, but I do see that we both value our kids and want the best for them." We may not agree with how we're going to get there, but we do want the same thing for our children. The same is true for other loaded issues. Remember, you're on the same side, the side of the marriage. There will be moments when you must rise above your strong convictions and agree to disagree for the greater good. It will require both of you to meet in the middle and hopefully find common ground about the issue. But often, just validating each other's perspectives, even if you disagree, is enough. The most important question to ask is "How will this affect our connection and our relationship?"

3. Sit in their seat.

Instead of assuming your way is the *right* way, or your number is the *right* number, try seeing the world from your spouse's perspective. In other words, have some empathy.

Empathy is about getting on your spouse's level and feeling it *with* them. Punctuality is a ten for Meygan and only a four for Casey. Because of that, he usually swings Meygan's way, but it's often still a sticking point. Casey's lack of punctuality used to make Meygan insane. To him, being "on time" wasn't about respect—it was just a fluid concept. As a girl, Meygan had to grow up super fast; she looked for safety and predictability everywhere she could find it. It's the source of her love of planning and control, and it's why timeliness is a ten for her.

Casey has worked on being on time. Meanwhile, Meygan has also come to realize it's not a personal attack when Casey is late to a doctor's appointment or dinner, just a different way of seeing the world. Because, let's be honest, as much as he tries to work on it, Casey will be late again. We can compromise and give a little and let things go, but we know we're not going to change anybody's innate personality here. Erring on the side of curiosity about your spouse, instead of judgment, is helpful for creating that empathy. Learning more about your partner's story and the need behind the emotion builds understanding.

4. Choose love—even when it's hard.

Like we said in part 1, love isn't just a feeling—it's a choice. Sometimes the most loving thing you can do is to stop trying to control your spouse and start appreciating what they bring to the table. It means admiring and accepting them instead of saying things like "What were you thinking?" or "Why can't you just be different?" or "Why can't you just be more like me?" Has that tactic ever worked for your marriage? Of course not. And you'd hate for your spouse to say that to you. Choosing love looks like letting certain things go, having compassion for your spouse, and making an effort when you know it really, really matters to them. It takes courage and vulnerability. And it's the best thing you can do for your marriage.

5. Focus on your similarities.

Instead of noticing only your differences, take time to celebrate what you do have in common. We are both competitive, so we make a point to play games together regularly. It's a small thing, but it reminds us that at the core, we're still a team.

Look through the ideas in the previous chapter about fun. That's a great place to start when remembering your similarities. What did you do when you were dating? Did you both love disc golf? A certain podcast? A dumb TV show from ages ago? We're sure you have more in common than that. But if you're in an especially tough period of your marriage, start by remembering the interests that used to connect you. This perspective shift alone can soften those rough edges caused by feeling like you've grown apart.

6. Leverage your differences to be stronger together.

We said at the beginning that your differences aren't meant to be just managed but celebrated and leveraged. They can be your superpower. Here are some examples of what that looks like in practice.

Introvert vs. Extrovert
One thrives on quiet. One thrives on connection.
Together: You create space and spark.

Planner vs. Go with the Flow
One keeps things organized. The other keeps things fun.
Together: You create a balance between structure and spontaneity.

On Time vs. Late
One values punctuality. The other moves at their own
    pace.
Together: You create a balance between reliability and
    flexibility.

Early Bird vs. Night Owl
One starts strong. One finishes strong.
Together: You can cover more ground in a day.

Spender vs. Saver
One values experiences. One values security.
Together: You can create a budget that honors both.

Fighter vs. Flighter
One pushes toward resolution. One likes space to process.
Together: You learn when to engage and when to pause.

Thinker vs. Feeler
One thinks clearly. One feels deeply.
Together: You lead with heart and wisdom.

Meygan still hates to cook. But Casey still loves to eat, so he
learned to cook for himself. He's regularly grateful for the structure and stability Meygan brings to his overly optimistic, idea-
filled, ADHD-riddled life. And Casey's spontaneity, which drove
Meygan crazy for so long, is what keeps their lives and marriage
fun, adventurous, and joyful. We didn't really change, but our
perspectives did.

Your differences aren't meant to divide you—they're meant to
balance you. When you learn to appreciate them, you'll realize
that the person you married isn't *wrong* for you. They're the person who makes life richer, fuller, and—yes—sometimes a little
crazier. Maybe that's exactly how it should be.

CONNECTING QUESTIONS

1. Do you believe opposites attract? Why or why not?

2. What is one thing you were attracted to in me when we were dating because it was different from you?

3. When we got married, did you think we were more similar or more different and why?

4. What is one area where our differences are a good thing because we balance each other out?

5. In what ways can we become a better team by working with our differences?

HABIT 7

The Code Word

You're still gonna fight. Learn to fight fair.

———•————————————————————•———

Every single couple who comes to see us, or goes to therapy, or stays up late-night googling, or files for divorce does it because of some version of the same reason: conflict. We're willing to bet it's at least part of why you picked up this book. Conflict is when you and your spouse have different needs, opinions, or expectations, and those differences clash. It's what keeps marriage therapists in business. And, needless to say, conflict gets a bum rap in relationships.

We'll admit it. We both came into marriage thinking that if we fought, it meant something was wrong with us. But in this chapter, we're going to offer you a new way to think about conflict. As with differences, it's not something you can get rid of. Likely, you'll always experience it in your relationship.

At its core, conflict is just a difference of perspective. It's two people coming into a moment with different expectations—and clashing as a result. You and your spouse are talking, sharing, maybe trying to make a decision, and suddenly you realize you don't see eye to eye on something. You expected them to agree with you, and they didn't. You expected them to help, and they didn't. You don't care about clothes, and your blood pressure rises when they come home with an expensive outfit. So far, all those scenarios are completely normal.

But what happens next? If we don't have the right conflict skills, things can quickly shift from discussion to combat. You start fighting dirty. The name-calling, defensiveness, silent treatment, or criticisms start flying. And if things get bad enough, one or both of you might even decide to go for the jugular. Hit the other where it hurts. Worst-case scenario, you end up in a stand-off with nobody giving an inch and nowhere to go. So you give up, and nothing good comes of it. That's how *not* to fight. All of us probably know how to do that already. (And some of us are *pros*.)

It doesn't have to be that way. Conflict is inevitable when two people are navigating life with different backgrounds, personalities, values, expectations, and triggers. However, if handled correctly, conflict can be one of the greatest tools for strengthening your marriage. You heard that right. Conflict can be *good*. Here's why:

1. *Conflict gives you a chance to express your needs, desires, and preferences.* It's a chance to get something off your chest and learn more about each other. You know that inkling you feel when you're both approaching the precipice of "Uh-oh, we might be on opposite sides of this one" and you're unsure what's going to happen? It can be a good sign. You're about to express something important to you. And so will your spouse. Learning about each other is always a good thing.

2. *It helps you better understand each other's strengths, if you listen well, which allows you to lean on each other.* Remember, you're very different people and you have

different strengths. Conflict is a place where you can highlight that in a good way.

3. *It builds intimacy.* Nothing strengthens a relationship—any relationship—like working through a conflict together. If you can work through conflict and come out on the other side stronger, it proves your commitment to each other. It's easy to be loving when you're agreeing with each other. It's harder when you are on opposite sides of an issue. That's what makes working through it so meaningful.

4. *It motivates you to keep fighting for your marriage.* After you resolve conflict, you have a newfound confidence in your relationship. You can weather the hard stuff. You can overcome. Nothing can take you down. It also creates momentum. You can do this because you've done it before. Conflict loses some of its power and becomes less scary.

FROM CONFLICT TO COMBAT

Our past experiences shape how we handle conflict. If you grew up in a home where disagreements meant yelling and slamming doors, you might instinctively avoid fights (like Casey). Or (like Meygan) maybe the fact that your family ignored every issue, stuffing it way down deep, and would then blow up at the most random times has created the instinct in you to address everything, all the time, immediately, so you know where everyone stands. Our upbringings—and how they integrate into our conflict styles—are unique to each of us.

Biology plays a role too. Here's what happens when you're in conflict. It all starts with the brain's response to stress. When we feel threatened—whether it's by a tiger in the wild or a passive-aggressive "whatever" from our spouse—our brains jump into fight-or-flight mode. The amygdala (the part of the brain responsible for processing emotions) hijacks our rational thinking, making us more reactive and defensive. That's why it's so easy to go from calmly discussing who should pick up dinner to screaming at each other.

When this happens, you've officially entered combat. Your blood starts pumping, your heart starts racing, you remember every negative thing your spouse has ever done, and you want to yell or hide or whatever your defensive mechanism of choice may be. In short: You're triggered. What we mean is that you're flooded with emotions. The emotions are so many, and so overpowering, that you can't think rationally anymore. You're about to be controlled by your base instincts, which will almost certainly lead you to make the situation worse. The fighters will fight and the flighters will flight (amiright?). And if you're in a marriage with one fighter and one flighter, you're coping in exactly opposite ways. We polled our audience a few years ago, asking whether they deal with fight responses or flight responses in their marriages. Eight thousand people responded, and 71 percent said they're in a marriage with one of each.

This, right here, is where we get into trouble. We know you don't want to hurt each other. But when you're flooded, it's almost impossible not to. You're only human. To avoid going from conflict to combat, you're going to push a big ole hypothetical flashing red button that we call the code word.

THE CODE WORD

Pick a word, any word, or a short phrase. It could be "pineapple pizza" or "pink flamingo" or "Chaz needs a walk." Really anything. Bonus points if it makes you giggle a little, to take some of the steam out of the impending train wreck. When things get heated, someone says it, and it serves as a warning sign. "I need a time-out or things are going to get bad." It's a flashing red neon light that means "I love you enough to stop you here, because I don't want to say something I regret." Then you both do just that. You walk away to calm down. No other words are said after the code word. But listen up, flighters, we aren't flighting! We're just taking a temporary adult time-out. And fighters, we're not abandoning the fight! We're just giving ourselves some time so we don't hit below the belt.

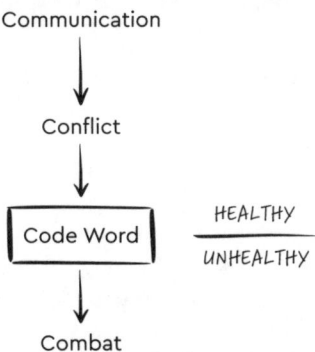

This break should last at least twenty minutes, but it can be longer. A good rule of thumb is no more than twenty-four hours. It allows each of you to regulate your emotions again and return to the conversation in a calmer state. It's especially useful for couples who regularly get stuck in negative patterns during arguments. When you're emotionally flooded and returning to your old ways, sometimes a pause is all you need to remember the "rules" and that you're on the same team.

As you go your separate ways, do something to calm your body and nervous system and get out of that fight-or-flight response. Go for a walk or a drive, read a chapter of a (chill) book, journal, do some yoga, stretch, pray, work out, take a shower.

Then, here's the important next step: It's the responsibility of the person who used the code word to bring the conversation up again. Lots of couples find it helpful to text each other something like "I was able to cool off and wanted to check in and see if you're ready to talk again. I'm here when you're ready." We al-ways recommend texting, or checking in digitally, from afar, in-stead of in person. If your partner is not ready to talk again, more interaction could worsen or re-escalate the situation.

MEYGAN'S INSIGHT

Here are some more examples of texts you could send:

"I've been able to calm down and I'm ready to talk when-ever you are."

"I'm ready to be open-minded and finish our conversation. Let me know when you're ready."

"I care about us and I'd like to work through this together. I'm ready to talk whenever you feel comfortable."

"I'm in a better headspace now and I'm ready to listen and talk things through. No pressure—just let me know when you're up for it."

You'll know you're ready when you no longer want to fight or flee. Do a quick self-check. Is your mind clear? Have your heart rate and breathing slowed down? Are your muscles relaxed, and has your tunnel vision receded? Then you're ready to re-engage. And if your spouse is not ready, please respect that. Give them the time they need. Don't push it.

Here are a few quick code word ground rules: It should never be used in normal conversation when you're not flooded. It's not an excuse to end a conversation you don't like. And it's definitely not a punishment for bad behavior. It should never be used to hurt the relationship more. It's only ever a safeguard to protect you both from each other and the instincts you have when your emotions take over. It's about prioritizing your relationship.

This habit has been incredibly helpful for a particular couple we work with. We'll call them Josh and Amy. Amy is a flighter. In conflict, she stuffs things way down deep; instead of pushing in, she pulls out. But this can only work for so long. After stewing in anger and irritation, Amy goes off the rails. Everything she has been holding in comes out way meaner than she intended because she's flooded, and Josh gets extra hurt because he loves words of affirmation and is sensitive to that kind of attack. Can you see the problem here? Recipe for disaster.

On month two of coaching, we taught them about the code word. It took another month to figure out how to use it in a way that worked for them, but pretty soon they were pros. It was usually Josh who invoked it. Which, by the way, is a pattern you may notice: One partner is likely better at reaching for this tool. (Casey is the one in our marriage.) Josh would notice that Amy was flooded and about to say something hurtful, and he'd say the code word. After a few weeks, this transformed the way they handled conflict. No more lashing out and bringing up unrelated wounds.

Now, after you've calmed down and come back to talk, there are a few key pieces of the conversation to get right. Let's walk through how to do it.

THE CONFLICT CONVERSATION

Whether you're coming back after invoking the code word or addressing a long-simmering conflict, we're about to show you a new way to talk about it. You *can* rewire the way you respond to conflict. We always say that learning how to fight right is about learning how to fight naked. And no, we're not talking about clothes being optional (though, hey—go for it!). Fighting naked means being emotionally vulnerable with each other—able to disagree but still feel safe, loved, and accepted.

This means no armor. No hiding behind a shield. No weapons. It means saying things like this:

- "I feel hurt" instead of "You always do this."
- "I need reassurance" instead of "You never make me feel secure."
- "I'm scared I'm slowly losing you" instead of "You don't care about me."

Imagine a world in which every couple could argue and still walk away feeling closer. That's what we're going to teach you.

Being emotionally vulnerable during an argument is terrifying. It requires trust, and it forces us to acknowledge our own fears and insecurities. But it's also the key to experiencing deeper intimacy and letting conflict make your relationship stronger. When you can be honest about your needs without attacking your spouse, you create a safe space for real connection.

We recommend always doing a self-check before you engage in an argument. Start by taking a moment to regulate your emotions and consider your approach. (If you don't feel regulated, it is not the time to approach.) Try asking yourself these three questions:

- Am I in the right headspace to have this conversation?
- Have I processed my emotions enough to communicate effectively?
- What is my goal in bringing up this issue? (For example: Do you want your spouse to listen and be a safe place to vent? Do you want an apology? Are you needing validation?)

The idea here is to make sure you're clearheaded and can follow the "rules" we're about to share. There's no fighting just for the sake of fighting. No bringing up an issue just to piss off your spouse. There's no shame in realizing it's not the right time, that you're not in the right mindset. It happens to all of us! Casey knows to never engage in conflict when he's hungry. No matter how much he might want to resolve things peacefully, if he's hungry, things will end badly for everyone. Know thyself. Are you upset about something at work that will affect this conversation? Have you had enough sleep? Your relationship is too precious and important to step into an argument when you might say something you don't mean just because you're tired.

THE FIVE "DON'TS" OF CONFLICT

All right, let's break it down and start with what *not* to do when officially engaging in a conflict-driven conversation. You might have seen some of these before, but they're worth revisiting before we go further.

1. Don't minimize your partner's feelings.

Let's say your spouse starts sharing something, and you respond with "Get over it" or "It's not a big deal." The intention might be good—you're trying to be a cheerleader and reassure them. But it invalidates their feelings. It says, "What you feel doesn't matter to me." No one wants to be told their emotions are insignificant when they're opening up. It minimizes what they're feeling. Stay away from that. Chances are, they'll share less and less over time because they believe you think their feelings aren't that important.

CASEY'S COACHING CORNER

This is a vicious cycle I see a lot. One person is constantly asking their partner to engage and open up. When that doesn't happen, they get exasperated and critical words come out. It becomes a self-fulfilling prophecy because the flighter or avoider no longer feels safe enough to talk with a critical spouse. In order to get out of this toxic merry-go-round, both partners need to recognize their role in it. The avoider is leaving their partner carrying the weight of the relationship, while the fighter needs to recognize how their words have pushed their partner away, which is the exact opposite of what they intended in the first place.

2. Don't avoid the conflict.

Some people avoid conflict because it triggers deep fears—like abandonment or rejection. Others avoid it because it feels uncomfortable, or they'd rather disengage than risk failing at resolution. But avoiding conflict leaves a relationship full of assumptions and unresolved tension. It's like death by a thousand paper cuts. You cannot avoid it forever. Might as well deal with it now.

3. Don't judge.

Meygan used to be a pro at judging. When Casey did something different from the way she would have done it, her immediate thought was *That's stupid. My way is the right way.* And that judgment—whether spoken aloud or rolling around in your head—shuts down connection. (By the way, even if you're just thinking something, that doesn't mean you're hiding it. We promise. Your spouse can tell.) Your partner won't want to open up if they feel judged every time they do. Conflict should create space for curiosity, not condemnation. Some of the things they say won't make sense to you, and vice versa. That's fine. You don't have to fully understand them to validate and empathize with them.

4. Don't stack the deck.

Have you ever started arguing about one thing, and suddenly, your partner is listing *everything* you've ever done wrong? That's stacking the deck—bringing up past grievances instead of focusing on the issue at hand. It's overwhelming, unproductive, and often a sign of unaddressed resentment. If past issues keep resurfacing, they probably need to be resolved individually, not dumped into every argument.

5. Don't be mean.

This sounds obvious, right? And yet, in the heat of the moment, it's easy to let name-calling, cussing, or belittling slip out. But fighting dirty damages trust and intimacy. If conflict means your partner has to brace themselves for meanness, of course they'll start avoiding it. You would too. Hurtful words aren't easily forgotten, and they chip away at your marriage over time.

THE FIVE "DOS" OF CONFLICT

Now here's what you *should* do in the conversation.

1. Assume positive intent.

Most people don't wake up thinking, *How can I make my spouse miserable today?* Working with couples in crisis, we've discovered that 99.999999 percent of the time, across the board, people are doing the best they can with the skills they have. If you assume your partner isn't trying to hurt you but is just responding with what they know, it shifts your mindset from defensiveness to curiosity and empathy. Their concerns become your concerns. We guarantee, they aren't trying to hurt you. On the contrary, they love you. And while we all make mistakes and do hurt each other, it's almost never on purpose. Don't assume the worst about your partner. That's a surefire way to end up in combat.

2. Listen with empathy.

This means putting down distractions, making eye contact, and truly trying to understand your spouse's experience. It's about listening to understand, not just waiting for your turn to talk. If your spouse feels truly heard, their defenses will drop, which makes the conversation more productive.

In our marriage, when we find ourselves in conflict, with a fight potentially brewing, Meygan's immediate instinct is to fix it. She wants to make a plan, create a list, take action—do something to take away the pain as quickly as possible. Most of the time Casey just wants her to listen.

It's hard—especially when you're flooded—but it's so, so important to hear the other person out and use language like "Thank you for sharing that. I appreciate that perspective." Fixers, hear this: Make eye contact, nod your head, be present, and shut your mouth. Then, watch your spouse's face relax and the conflict drift away. They don't need you to fix it. They just need you to listen and scream into the void later if you have to.

3. Use the "On a scale of one to ten" tactic.

Here it is again, another Caston favorite. We're all about emotional validation here. But we're also all about the practical. Not all issues are created equal. Sometimes an argument feels like a ten in the moment, but when you ask "How important is this to you on a scale of one to ten?" and you're honest with yourself, it turns out to be a three. This question helps put things in perspective, as we discussed in the chapter on leveraging your differences. This is a good one to use right in the heat of the moment. Like a blast of cold air, it can take the temperature down a bit.

If you're the more emotional one in the relationship, it can feel to your partner like everything is intense. It's overwhelming to them, and sometimes your tone and expression can make a feeling seem bigger than it is. They might get the impression that everything is a ten.

On the contrary, if you are often even-keeled and less emotional, your partner might not immediately understand the gravity of what you're communicating. They might assume this is just a two for you, when really it's an eight. Before things escalate, rate the issue for each other. This gives the less expressive person a chance to speak up and not be overshadowed by the communication of their more feelings-based partner.

4. Validate your partner's emotions.

Validation is the ultimate de-escalator. Recognizing and affirming how your spouse feels—without trying to fix or dismiss it—builds trust and connection. You cannot argue about how someone feels. What they are feeling is never wrong; it just is. So much of conflict boils down to one person wanting the other to confirm that they're heard and believed. Often this is all that needs to be "done." We know, it's easier said than done if you're feeling defensive or wronged. (We're going to dig into apologizing in the next chapter.) For now, here are some good phrases to use to validate your partner's emotions:

- "I hear you."
- "I validate that."
- "That makes sense."
- "I understand."
- "I hear you saying . . ."

5. Take responsibility.

Nothing defuses conflict faster than genuine accountability. Again, we're going to dig into how to apologize next. But here's a preview: A proper apology doesn't sound like "I'm sorry you feel that way." It's "I'm sorry for what I did. I see how it hurt you, and I want to make it better." Like we said at the beginning, most of our hurts are unintentional. When you take responsibility, you're not admitting to being a bad person or doing anything on purpose. You're accepting the situation and communicating that you want to make it right. There's freedom in this. We all make mistakes. Be accountable for your actions and let your spouse know that you're committed to doing things differently.

[Conflict caveat: Remember the four A's—abuse, affairs, addiction, and abandonment. If you are experiencing any of these in your marriage, there's a good chance that your conflict is beyond the scope of this chapter and the apologizing and forgiveness chapters. Those are serious issues that endanger you physically and emotionally. If you are experiencing these, seek outside help and prioritize your safety over everything first.]

Let's put all this conflict advice to use with an example. Marriage365 relies on the use of social media. We are always inundated with Instagram messages, so the two of us are on our phones a lot. There were several times recently when Casey looked over at Meygan during family time and saw that she was on her phone. Once or twice wasn't a big deal, but it was happening enough times that Casey started to feel unimportant. He could feel his irritation rising, stemming from the fact that when Meygan was face down in her phone, he didn't feel like a priority.

So on a night when he was feeling calm and clearheaded about it, he addressed it. He approached Meygan and told her that he'd been feeling frustrated and hurt lately by how much she'd been on her phone. Meygan could have immediately responded with defensiveness and tried to minimize Casey's feelings. "Things have been busy with the business lately! Of course that means more phone time! You should understand that and just get over it! Why do you need my attention all the time?" She could have easily turned that conflict into combat. In the short term, it might have even felt cathartic. But, of course, knowing what we know and having worked on this for a long time, Meygan didn't do that. Even if she felt justified in being on her phone, Casey *was* her priority. She didn't want to hurt him. And his feelings were valid. If she minimized them, that would only hurt him further and make things worse.

Meygan immediately owned her actions, apologized, and reaffirmed that their marriage was the most important thing to her. More important than social media or even the business. As much as she wanted to give an excuse, or even an explanation, that wasn't the time to do it. If you want to offer an explanation for your actions, do so later, not in the moment when your spouse brings up an issue.

That night, Meygan asked what she could do to make it right, and we brainstormed solutions together. It doesn't always go this well. We still mess this up. But on the good days, when we manage to let conflict make us stronger, this is how it looks.

If you start implementing the code word and these dos and don'ts of fighting, you will see a huge shift in your relationship pretty quickly. Even if you're doing this on your own. If your spouse isn't reading this book with you, you can still implement many of these tactics in your relationship. Your spouse will lose their sparring partner, and that's a big wake-up call. When you're soothing your own anger, refusing to engage in meanness, and not going into combat, there's not much they can do. Their defenses will come down as they feel heard and validated. It's hard work, we know. But that's the beauty of fighting fair.

We've said it before, and we'll say it again. The truest truth in marriage is this: If you want to make a better marriage, make a better you. The way you handle conflict is the way you love—so fight fair, fight naked, and fight for your marriage.

●━━━━━━━━━━━━●

CONNECTING QUESTIONS

1. When we have conflict, do you tend to fight (push in) or flee (pull away)? Why do you think that is?

2. How did your family handle conflict when you were growing up, and how do you see that impacting our relationship?

3. What are some early signs that you're feeling overwhelmed or shutting down during a disagreement?

4. What do you think should be our code word or code phrase to use when one of us is triggered?

5. What are some healthy things we can do separately once the code word has been said to help us cool off (e.g., go for a drive, pray, journal, work out, take a shower)?

Unsolicited Apologies

The magic wand of marriage.

———————•———————•———————

We all know about apologizing, right? You probably first learned to say sorry as a tiny child, when you whacked your brother over the head for taking your Goldfish crackers. Since before we can remember, we've been told that we should apologize when we hurt others. And yet, in our experience, the majority of adults are absolutely, spectacularly bad at it.

The main reasons people get apologies wrong are ego and defensiveness. Even if you do manage to get out the words "I'm sorry," all their power is canceled by the words you say before and after. Many people overexplain what they did and why they did it. Maybe you want to justify your actions and make it clear that you didn't mean to hurt your spouse. You might even have had an understandable reason for whatever happened. AND an apology is not the time to get into that. There actually *is* a correct process you can follow, an exact script even, to apologize correctly and heal (sometimes decades-old) wounds. More on that in a minute.

In every relationship, there's often a gap between what we intend and the impact our actions have on our partner. And here's the most important part: Impact outweighs intent. While it's important to help your spouse understand your actions, it's more important to acknowledge how those actions made them feel. That's why the phrase "I didn't mean to" or "I didn't mean it that way" falls so flat. For the purposes of apologizing, what you meant doesn't matter. How it made them feel does. There will be time later to explain yourself and talk through intentions. But not while you apologize.

At least half our time in coaching sessions with couples or in intensives is spent walking couples through offering each other apologies, because it is so powerful. If you're experiencing disconnection in your relationship, an apology is the best way to reconnect. It's not a kind gesture or a gift or make-up sex, though those are all good ideas. These simple words have the power to vanish resentment and erase the mental load of anxiety or sadness that someone carries because of a hurt we caused. An apology is the closest thing marriage has to a magic wand.

Here's how this often goes. Over time, in your relationship, you both overpromise and underdeliver. They're late for the seventh time. You didn't stand up to your parents in front of your spouse. They said something mean. You said something sarcastic. There's a slight, a little insult, an unkind word, a rude look, a minor indifference, and on it goes. Sometimes there is something BIG—but we've found, more often than not, that these smaller things add up over time. We need a way to start taking some of those accumulated pains off your marriage plate.

THE POWER OF AN UNSOLICITED APOLOGY

When we were in those terrible first few years of our marriage, it was Meygan who started to get help first. We'll tell that whole story in the final chapter. Meygan started going to counseling alone because Casey wouldn't go with her at the beginning. She began working on herself. There were no guarantees that working on herself would result in a better marriage, but it was all she could control, and she hoped and prayed for the best.

As a result of Meygan addressing her faults head-on, she started cultivating one of the most powerful habits in this book. Ultimately, this was the thing that moved Casey enough to decide he wanted to change as well. That habit is the unsolicited apology.

Casey had mentioned multiple times, over many years, that he felt like Meygan tried to control too many aspects of his life. She would correct behaviors she didn't like, force him to handle conflict like she did, and criticize how he spent money. During therapy, Meygan created a list of what she knew she needed to apologize for. At the top was her control issues. So one day, out of the blue, she said, "You know, I'm really sorry I've tried to control you so much, making you feel disrespected and guarded. I know what hurt you, and you don't deserve that. I'm going to be actively working on this moving forward."

In a marriage whose well-worn patterns involved screaming and fighting, this was revolutionary. In fact, it was so unlike any other occurrence in our relationship that Casey was suspicious at first. He thought, *Who are you, and what have you done with my wife?* After a few more of these unsolicited apologies, though, Casey started to soften. To make a very, very long story very, very short: He also started apologizing, and we both began to change. There's so much more to it, but the change in our marriage started with voluntarily admitting our faults. That's what got the flywheel going. It created the momentum for all the healing that came next.

Here's why the unsolicited apology is so powerful. When you apologize for something before your spouse asks you to—before they have to drag it out of you like a toddler being pulled from the playground—it shows you're self-aware. Every human messes up. That's just a fact. We say impulsive things, we have bad days, we get selfish, we allow our anger to win, and sometimes, we just get plain lazy and end up hurting the people we love. Like we said before, nobody wakes up thinking, *Today, I'm going to make my spouse absolutely miserable.* (If you do, we have bigger problems to discuss.) And yet, whether intentional or not, hurt happens. You've messed up. You do have things to apologize for. And so does your spouse, by the way.

Let's just address the elephant in the book: It might suck at first to apologize without your spouse reciprocating. Especially if you feel like you are the most wronged in the relationship. But that's not the point just yet. This is about you. Emotionally healthy people own their behaviors and examine what part they've played in their situation. Sometimes we do have to ask for apologies, and in healthy marriages that's received well. But if apologizing isn't a habit in your marriage yet, you need to start before you're asked.

MEYGAN'S INSIGHT

I have never once regretted being the bigger and better person in my marriage. It's super tough in the moment, but in hindsight, I'm always glad I did it. I'd rather it be me who apologizes first than sit around and hope Casey does. I want to own my mistakes, learn from them, make things right, and move on.

The unsolicited apology is an absolute game changer for your marriage. Take a minute to imagine this. How would it feel if someone who wronged you, even years ago, came up and voluntarily apologized and showed you how much they understood how their actions affected you? Whoa. That'd feel really good, right? It'd probably heal something deep in you. An unsolicited apology validates your feelings, shows they're taking responsibility, and signals that they genuinely *care* about making things right. It's a way of saying, "I see the impact of my actions, and I want to repair the damage." In short: It's magic. That kind of apology is healing. It softens hearts. It rebuilds trust.

Another great use of the unsolicited apology is when you've already formally apologized for something—usually something big. Here's what we mean. A while back, we worked with a couple who were rebuilding their relationship after the husband had an affair. Six months earlier he'd offered a thorough, heartfelt apology and done a lot of work to repair their marriage. On the whole, the wife was receptive to it. But she admitted in one of our sessions that she still struggled with anger and resentment every now and then.

At first, the husband pulled the classic "But I already apologized. . . ." as if that washed away the hurt of an affair once and for all. To his credit, with some self-reflection, he started to regularly offer unsolicited apologies for the pain he inflicted. Even though he'd already done it, even though the affair had happened six months ago, even though he wished she was "over it," the truth was she wasn't over it. Just as she felt lingering pain, he wanted to show that he still regularly felt regret. Voluntarily, he would offer up, "Hey, I'm so sorry I betrayed you and hurt you deeply. I was such a fool, but I want you to know that I love you and I'm committed to you." That's all it takes. Sometimes, with our biggest mistakes, we have to apologize more than once. And someone has to go first. Take initiative and let it be you.

CASEY'S COACHING CORNER

There is a common misconception about offering an apology to your spouse without prompting. It goes something like this: "Why would I bring up a painful issue from our past when we are connecting right now? Wouldn't that make her sad and make the relationship worse?" Wrong. What it actually shows your partner is that you are considerate of the pain they carry and you want to validate them. It quickens the healing process and deepens the relationship because your partner feels like you really see them.

THE WORST APOLOGIES EVER
(AND WHY THEY SUCK)

Here are the most common mistakes we see when people apologize. Even if you have the best of intentions, when you issue the following sucky apologies, they fall short. They miss the real point of an apology, which is to own your mistakes, show remorse, and make it right. If you're guilty of any of the following apology disasters, don't worry—you're in good company. But it's time to retire these phrases once and for all.

1. The "I'm Sorry You Feel That Way" Apology

This is not an apology; it's a Jedi mind trick to make the other person feel like they're overreacting. Saying, "I'm sorry you feel that way" shifts the responsibility away from you and onto your spouse's emotions. Imagine if your spouse ran over your foot with the car and, instead of apologizing, said, "I'm sorry your foot hurts." That would not go over well. A heartfelt apology is not about manipulating your partner or trying to make them feel a certain way. It doesn't matter if you feel like their hurt is "valid." The point is they're hurt. That's all that matters.

2. The "But" Apology

"I'm sorry for yelling at you, *but* you were being difficult." The moment you say "but," you erase everything that came before it. The word *but* is just a sneaky way of saying, "Here's why this isn't actually my fault." A real apology stands on its own. If you use the word *but* when you apologize, I'm sorry, BUT it doesn't count. Sorry not sorry.

MEYGAN'S INSIGHT

My default is to explain myself, hoping Casey will understand where I was coming from. But I've learned that in the middle of an apology, it can come across as just making excuses. This is especially tough for people like me who can be a little stubborn or set in our ways—it feels unnatural to just own a mistake without defending it.

3. The Repeat Offender Apology

This is when someone apologizes over and over for the same behavior but never actually puts energy toward changing. Apologies without changed behavior are just manipulation. If you're saying sorry for the fifth time about the same issue, it's time to ask yourself, *Do I really mean it?* Your spouse already thinks you don't. (Ask us how we know . . .) Words without actions mean nothing.

4. The Dramatic Overcorrection

We love passion, but let's not be too extra. Saying, "I'm the worst person alive, I don't deserve your love, I'll just go live in a cave now" is not helpful or true. Your spouse doesn't want you to self-destruct—they just want you to acknowledge your mistake and work on it. Self-pity isn't necessary, attractive, or mature. Clear and meaningful beat dramatic every time.

THE FOUR-STEP APOLOGY

Okay, let's dig into how to apologize the right way. A real, meaningful apology requires intention, accountability, and action. Because, hear this loud and clear, apologies are for *others*, not us.

You might have felt extremely justified in what you did. You had your phone out at dinner because you were waiting for an important call. You yelled at your partner for being late because it was an important appointment. Maybe you believe you had a good reason. But the fact remains: They're hurt. And that's what matters here. We apologize for them because they're hurt. If you want to explain later why you did what you did to help them understand, that's fine. But it's never part of the apology. It's never an excuse. Enter: the four-step apology, a structured approach that ensures your apology is heard and helps repair the relationship. Not because you were right or wrong but because you love your spouse.

Step 1: "I'm sorry for [action] + [feeling]."

This is where you take full responsibility for your actions—without excuses, justifications, or deflecting blame. That's the key. A weak apology starts with something like "I'm sorry you feel that way" or "I didn't mean to upset you"—which isn't an apology at all. Instead, clearly state that you were wrong. Here are the magic words.

> Example:
> *"I'm sorry for speaking over you while we were talking today."*
> Not: "I'm sorry you felt ignored." (See the difference? One takes ownership; the other shifts responsibility onto the other person.)

Acknowledging the action is one thing, but recognizing its impact on the other person is what truly makes an apology meaningful. This is where empathy comes in—showing that you understand how your actions affected them emotionally, mentally, or even practically. Say, "I can see that my actions made you feel . . ."

Example:

> *"I can see how that made you feel unheard and frustrated, and I understand why that would be upsetting."*

Not: "I wasn't trying to hurt you." (Intent doesn't erase impact.)

Here is a list of examples of how to put these together:

I'm sorry for **spending too much time on my phone**, which made you feel **ignored**.

I'm sorry for **putting my career in front of our marriage**, which made you feel **neglected**.

I'm sorry for **yelling at you**, which made you feel **disrespected**.

I'm sorry for **walking away**, which made you feel **unimportant**.

I'm sorry for **calling you names**, which made you feel **worthless**.

I'm sorry that I **haven't initiated sex**, which made you feel **undesired**.

I'm sorry for **interrupting you**, which made you feel **overlooked**.

I'm sorry for **not helping around the house**, which made you feel **overwhelmed**.

I'm sorry for **spending more time with the kids than with you**, which made you feel **abandoned**.

I'm sorry I **haven't communicated my needs**, which made you feel **confused**.

I'm sorry I have **put my own wants and desires before yours**, which made you feel **invisible**.

I'm sorry I've **been controlling**, which made you feel **manipulated**.

I'm sorry I **lied to you**, which made you feel **deceived**.

I'm sorry I **was short with you**, which made you feel **irritated**.

I'm sorry I **didn't stand up for you**, which made you feel **humiliated**.

I'm sorry for **trying to fix you instead of listening to you**, which made you feel **disconnected**.

I'm sorry for **judging you**, which made you feel **ashamed**.

MEYGAN'S INSIGHT

There's a reason this formula works. Some other apology formulas are vague; this is intentionally clear and short. It helps those who struggle with articulation and intentionally doesn't allow you to elaborate. If the phrasing feels unnatural, you can manipulate the sentence structure a little. Like "I'm sorry for spending too much time on my phone. That made you feel ignored." But the contents of the apology remain exactly the same. Do not add to it; do not subtract from it.

Step 2: "I was wrong."

Now that you've named the action and validated your spouse's feelings, it's time to express sincere regret. This isn't about guilt or self-pity—it's about demonstrating that you truly feel bad and wish you had done things differently. There's power and freedom in admitting you were wrong. Do not blame; do not point fingers. Just say these powerful words: "I was wrong . . ."

This might be the hardest part for some people. But let us

help you save face here. You're not saying anything about your-self or your character. You're just apologizing for your actions—actions that hurt your partner. A core tenet of building trust is taking responsibility. You're taking responsibility for the feeling of pain you caused your loved one. That's what a mature and kind partner does.

> Example:
> *"I was wrong for making you feel that your input wasn't valuable."*
> *Not:* "I didn't think it was a big deal." (That just mini-mizes the issue.)

Step 3: "How can I make this better?"

A real apology doesn't stop at words—it includes action and problem-solving. This step is about committing to change and ensuring the hurt doesn't happen again. This is when you get to work as a team and brainstorm different ideas for actions you could take in the future. You want to ensure that the ideas or boundaries you come up with are realistic and clear. Stay away from things like "I'm going to listen more" or "I won't do it again." Ask what you can do to make amends or suggest a way to improve moving forward.

> Example:
> *"Moving forward, I'm going to turn off my phone Tuesdays and Thursdays by six o'clock so I can be more present with you and the kids."*
> *Not:* "I'll try to be on my phone less." (Vague promises don't rebuild trust.)
>
> *"Moving forward, we'll commit to doing the Weekly Marriage Business Meeting every Sunday night so we're on the same page about my schedule."*
> *Not:* "I'll try to communicate better."

"From now on, I'll ask you first before inviting my parents over, and we'll decide together what works for us."
Not: "I'll try to include you more when it comes to my parents."

"Every Saturday morning, I'll take the kids out so you can have a break and some alone time."
Not: "I'll start helping out more and giving you some alone time."

MEYGAN'S INSIGHT

Sometimes all your spouse will need is the validation and sincere apology. It might be okay if neither of you has ideas for step 3—what to do next time. If you're on the receiving end of this kind of apology, just reply with a simple "You apologizing and meaning it is all I need to make it better."

Step 4: "Will you forgive me?"

This is what brings everything full circle. If you're the partner apologizing, simply say, "Will you forgive me?"

No example needed here. Just ask the question. That's it.

Forgiveness can be a longer and more complex process than just telling someone you forgive them. And we'll get into how to actually forgive in more detail in the next chapter. For now, just know that you should always ask for forgiveness at the end of an apology, and when you're the one being asked, you should say yes only if you really mean it.

If you're the person being apologized to, it's totally fine to say you need some more time to process. But know that the ball is now in your court and you need to circle back. If you say you've forgiven your spouse but you're still walking around hurt and bitter, it's confusing to them. They think you've resolved the

How to Start an Apology

You made a mistake . . . now what? It's time to give a four-step proper apology, and we've given you a jump start to step 1.

Remember the four steps are:

STEP 1

I'm sorry for _(ACTION)_ + _(FEELING)_ .

STEP 2

I was wrong!

STEP 3

How can I make this better?

STEP 4

Will you forgive me?

issue because you expressly told them you did. It's not fair to say it if you don't mean it.

This framework ensures your apology is more than just a formality. It fosters healing and growth. When people feel genuinely heard and respected, they're far more likely to move forward with trust intact. So next time you mess up (because, let's face it, you will), use the four-step apology. Own it, mean it, and back it up with action. That's how you repair relationships—not with empty words, but with real accountability. And bonus points if you do it unprompted.

The four-step apology isn't just for your spouse; it's a habit that can transform *every* important relationship in your life. And this habit is especially powerful if you can practice it with your kids. Think about it—how often did your parents sincerely apologize to you when they were wrong? If the answer is "not often," that probably explains why so many of us struggle with apologies now. When you apologize to your kids or let them watch you apologize to your spouse, you teach them that it's okay to make mistakes, that taking responsibility is a sign of strength, and that they can trust you to be honest, even when it's hard.

Instead of saying, "Sorry I yelled at you," say "Hey, I'm sorry for yelling at you this morning and making you feel scared. That wasn't okay. I was wrong, and I want to work on staying calm even when I'm frustrated. Can you forgive me?"

You'd be amazed at how this strengthens other relationships in your life. If you have a parent who's hurt you, especially one who hurt you over a long period of time or many years ago, can you imagine what it would feel like if they called you up and spontaneously apologized? What would you feel? Can you imagine the relief? The comfort and peace you would feel? The four-step apology works in any situation. It doesn't matter if you're apologizing to your spouse, your child, your best friend, or even the barista you were rude to because you hadn't had your coffee yet. Owning your mistakes makes you a better human, period. An unsolicited, sincere apology is one of the best gifts you can give your spouse. It shows you care, it shows maturity, and it starts the process of healing.

CONNECTING QUESTIONS

1. Growing up, did you ever see your parents give each other a sincere apology? Why or why not?

2. What do you think is the difference between a sincere and an insincere apology?

3. What actions or changes would help you trust that my apology is sincere?

4. How do you know when I am genuinely sorry versus just trying to smooth things over?

5. How can we create a habit of giving four-step apologies in a way that builds trust and strengthens our connection?

Head. Hands. Heart. Habit.

You've been told to forgive. We'll show you how.

━━━━━━━●━━━━━━━━━━━━━━━●━━━━━━━

In 1993, Mary Johnson's only child, Laramiun Byrd, was shot and killed at a party. He was twenty years old. Mary was at work when she received a call saying her son's body was at the morgue. She almost immediately blacked out. She doesn't remember leaving the building or the short ride downtown to her sister's house.

She learned that Laramiun had gotten into a fight that night with a teenager, an encounter that ended with Mary's son being shot four times. Three days after the murder, police picked up the suspect—Oshea Israel—and took him into custody. According to the Forgiveness Project, Mary said later in an interview, "I believe hate set in then and there." He was tried as an adult and sentenced to twenty-five years in prison. Mary was glad. She viewed him as an animal and wanted the worst for him. After he was put away, she thought she'd feel some sort of closure, but she didn't.

Over the years, Mary said, her hatred for Oshea eventually spread to others. She began to treat many people in her life with contempt. "The root of bitterness ran deep, anger had set in and

I hated everyone," she said. Her life was falling apart, not just because of the loss of her son, but because of the deep-seated disdain she had for the person who'd taken him. She was a woman of faith and knew she was called to forgive. But how could you forgive someone who'd done something like that? And why would you ever want to? They certainly wouldn't deserve it.

Eventually, she realized that she couldn't live with this burden anymore. She'd never been to a prison, but she went to confront Oshea and say what she needed to say. They spoke for two hours. He admitted what he'd done and clearly regretted his actions. At the end of their meeting, they hugged, and he walked back to his cell in handcuffs. Mary said, "As I got up, I felt something rising from the soles of my feet and leaving me. . . . It was over." She'd genuinely forgiven Oshea.

Forgiveness. That's what finally set Mary free. When Oshea got out of prison in 2010, Mary helped him find housing in her neighborhood, and they went on to be neighbors. They regularly shared their story with the public to honor Laramiun and show others the power of forgiveness. "Unforgiveness is like cancer," Mary said. "It will eat you from the inside out. . . . The forgiveness is for me."

If apologizing is what we do for others, forgiveness is what we do for ourselves. We covered apologizing in the previous chapter; here we'll cover forgiveness. But forgiving someone is about much more than just saying you've done it; it's a process you need to walk through. Forgiveness is not some kind of fairy dust that comes upon you and magically releases any pent-up bitterness.

So, how do you know when you need to forgive someone? And how do you know when you've actually forgiven? It starts with a self-check. The first thing to ask yourself is this: *Is there something I keep bringing up over and over? Do I replay past hurts or arguments regularly in my head?* That's the first sign that you haven't forgiven your spouse. We've all had those two-in-the-morning moments when we're ruminating on a situation and pondering how to retaliate. Is there something your partner did that you continually feel like you need to address? Maybe, if there's very deep-seated unforgiveness for something like an affair or abuse, just their general presence triggers you. We've worked with couples that get emotionally flooded during most should-be-normal interactions with their spouse. (And, um, hello, we were also one of those couples.) That's a telltale sign that you have some forgiving to do.

THE SECRET INGREDIENT TO REPAIR

Let's say you've acknowledged that you need to forgive your spouse for something. There is a nagging hurt that happened in the past but keeps impacting your present. If that's you, there are three ingredients for repair. The first is compassion. The second, ideally, is a four-step apology. (No, you won't always get one. We'll address that below.) The third is forgiveness. Your spouse can do everything right—apologize and change in every way you've asked—but if you don't forgive them, nothing will get better. If they said something hurtful a year ago, offered a sincere apology, and changed the way they speak to you, but you still ruminate on that painful comment and think about it often, the relationship is not repaired. You haven't forgiven them.

In order for you to walk through the steps of forgiveness, you need to find compassion for your spouse. What's going on in your spouse's world? Do you have any idea? Are they hurting? Are they under stress? Are they going through a difficult time with work or their health? Tap into that spousal awareness. Is there a difference between you that caused them to see that action completely differently? Maybe your spouse grew up in a house where showing emotion wasn't okay, and it really hurts you that they don't engage to the level you would like. But can you see why they'd do that? Why it makes sense to them? This never means the other person doesn't have to change; it just means we offer each other grace and the benefit of the doubt. Responding in love is tough when you're pissed, but stepping into each other's shoes is an act of love. And don't we all want that offered to us?

Compassion feels like putting on another lens. Not the lens of your pain, but the lens of your spouse. If you're reading this and you've been in an unforgiveness gridlock for years, seeing things from your spouse's perspective will be tough. You won't feel like doing it for them. You're probably desperate for them to try to see your side for once. But somebody has to go first. Try just examining it from their point of view, and see if that leads to a little compassion.

HOW TO FORGIVE

How will you know you've actually forgiven your spouse? The progression will look something like this. It'll start in your head. Okay, well, maybe you won't actually feel that one. Our heads are for thinking, not feeling. But that is where it starts—not in your heart. Because the truth is that you won't feel forgiveness right away. Before you can feel better, we have to do a little brain retraining.

In our heads, we often operate with a justice complex. An eye for an eye, right? You hit me, I hit back. You offer me a sarcastic comment, here's one right back at ya. Oftentimes, we even over-reciprocate and escalate the situation by hitting back harder. But responding in unkindness when you've been hurt will only make you feel worse. It'll make your burden heavier and weigh you down. It'll affect your sleep, your job, your relationships, and your parenting.

Forgiveness starts with your thoughts. We've found that one of the best ways to change these thoughts is to start writing down qualities about your spouse that you love. Again, this is especially true if you've been in a forgiveness gridlock. You need to remind yourself of your partner's good qualities and rehearse saying, "I'm choosing to forgive." Say it out loud if you need to. We encourage couples all the time to keep a journal and write down ten things every day that they love about the other. Keep it on your nightstand and force yourself to do it.

This is how we retrain our thoughts. Because, contrary to popular belief, we do have control over them. Your brain is running the show here—tell it what to focus on. This is one of the reasons why we love the 60-Second Blessing so much. It forces you to think and say positive things out loud, which might start as awkward and uncomfortable but actually rewires synapses in your innermost circuitry. It's not cheesy or woo-woo. It's neuroscience. The act of writing things down repeatedly strengthens neural pathways, especially in the brain's prefrontal cortex, which is responsible for decision-making and emotional regulation. You want to like your spouse more and find it easier to forgive? Write it down.

The next place forgiveness shows up is your hands. Or, more accurately, your actions. Here's the truth: People don't do what you tell them to do. They do what they tell *themselves* to do. If you begin tricking your brain and writing down positive thoughts about your spouse, you're going to respond accordingly. Full disclosure, though: This is probably the hardest step of forgiveness, because it's going to require you to love someone who doesn't deserve it. And that will feel unfair. It's waaaaay easier to love our spouse when they deserve it—when they're being loving back.

As you well know by now, Meygan gets annoyed when people are late. And Casey is late often, so she has plenty of opportunities to practice forgiveness on this front. She also knows that making him coffee is on Casey's Love List and tries to practice that regularly. But it's a heck of a lot easier when Casey hasn't just been late. When he has been late, Meygan's annoyed! *He's done it again! He knows how much it means to me, and still he keeps being late.* So getting up and making coffee for him the morning after is tough. She doesn't feel like it. And she certainly doesn't feel like bringing it to him in bed, which he *extra* likes. But this is what forgiveness in action looks like. It looks like doing it before you feel like it. First you think it; then you do something forgiving *before* you feel like it. And you know what? That response of love, after your spouse knows they've messed up, is a powerful thing. It shows them that they're allowed to be messy and they're loved just the same. They feel safe.

It may take a few months of offering your spouse compassion and rewriting your thoughts before you have the courage to start taking action. This is a process. Some days you'll be better at it than others. But once you do move through those first two places—head and hands—you'll start to feel it in your heart. (Cue a clip of the Grinch's heart growing three sizes that day!) If you've chosen love over pain—courage over comfort—you can confidently know that you have forgiven your spouse. You are choosing it, day after day, and that anger and resentment have subsided. Whether you receive something back or not, you're doing what you need to do, and you can feel the change in yourself.

From here, forgiveness can become a way of life for you. People hurt you, and you feel it and acknowledge it, without feeling forced to carry it. Forgiveness has become a habit, which is the fourth part of the process. Like all the marriage habits we cover, over time, you won't have to walk through these steps as consciously. You will know them, live them, breathe them. Those neural pathways will be so well worn, the actions will get easier. And in this habit, you get the chance to avoid one of the biggest pitfalls that keep people miserable and angry and grumbling about someone who wronged them thirty years ago. Keep short accounts. Loosen your grip. Let things go. This is about your freedom, not anyone else's.

Head = Thoughts

↓

Hands = Actions

↓

Heart = Feelings

↓

Habit = Rituals

Casey's Coaching Corner

We never feel like forgiving. You must make a conscious choice to forgive, which starts with your thoughts. Then you make a decision, which rewires your thinking and translates to your actions or reactions. Then as you show up in a healthy way, you start to feel good that you are doing the right thing. That's when you actually feel it in your heart. As you continually change your life through the power of forgiveness, this becomes the new ritual or habit of your relationship.

If I forgive them, do I have to forget?

Absolutely not. The bigger the pain, the more impossible forgetting will be. But as you forgive, it should take up less space in your brain. It should irritate and nag at you less. You shouldn't think about it all the time and want to rehash it. You don't have to forget, but you also shouldn't remember constantly. If you just had a big fight with your spouse last night, of course that will be on your mind. Give it time. You don't have to forget to take the trigger and emotion out of the event.

Meygan's Insight

It's important to understand that our brains aren't built to forget deep wounds—things like infidelity, addiction, or seasons of silence and disconnection leave a mark. We went through years of resentment and pain, and we haven't erased those memories. Truthfully, we probably never will. But here's the difference: They don't trigger us anymore, because we've made the choice to forgive each other and do the work to heal.

Doesn't forgiving them mean I'm condoning their actions?

Nope. Zero part of this process has to do with excusing behavior. You are justified in feeling disconnected if you've been hurt, especially if you've been hurt over and over again in the same ways after you've asked your partner to stop those actions. That kind of behavior is not okay. Your pain is valid.

And yet, your response matters. Laying down your pain doesn't have anything to do with condoning their actions. In fact, it doesn't have anything to do with them at all. They might not even know they've done anything wrong. No, this isn't about accepting bad behavior—it's about freeing yourself from a burden and moving forward.

Does my spouse have to say sorry or ask for forgiveness? Or, harder yet, what if they're not sorry?

The short answer is no. But let's dig into it because, many times in your marriage, you'll need to forgive without being asked or apologized to. Often, there's a good chance your spouse won't even know they did something wrong. Obviously, ideally, your spouse will be sorry and ask for forgiveness, even if you have to flat out tell them that they hurt you. Remember what we suggested in the Habit 7 chapter? Wait until you aren't triggered or emotionally flooded and address it. If your spouse knows you're in pain, in all likelihood they will be sorry and apologize. But there will be plenty of times when your differences or just life in general gets in the way and you hurt each other in normal, everyday, stupid ways that wear on your relationship over time. That's when you can offer unsolicited forgiveness. Forgiveness that wasn't asked for. And if you feel good enough about it in your own heart, you don't always have to bring it up.

If we map this onto other relationships in our lives, like our relationships with our parents, we know there's a good chance they won't ever ask for forgiveness. Those of us who have a mommy or daddy wound know deeply what this feels like. There's so much trauma and backstory from so long ago, the thought of your parent coming back after decades and apologizing . . . It's likely not going to happen. But that doesn't mean you can't forgive. You can still process forgiveness for yourself and offer it to them unsolicited. Think of the asking as just greasing the wheels. Sure, it makes things a lot easier. You're validated and on the same page. But when you don't get that apology, don't let it stop you from forgiving.

What do I do if they stop caring?

The opposite of love isn't hate; it's indifference. It's when you actually stop caring. We've counseled many people who come to us and use the exact language that their spouse "doesn't care" about them or the relationship. There's a chance that's true, but don't assume it at first. Many behaviors look like apathy, but they aren't. Your spouse could be an avoider, experiencing emotional overload. They could be conflict averse or a people pleaser, or they might genuinely believe you're fine. In most cases, we've found that the partner truly does care—their actions may just be sending the opposite message.

But sometimes it is true. If your marriage really doesn't matter to them anymore, or the pain they're inflicting is too great for you, it's time to reevaluate things. You'll still want to offer forgiveness—that's always necessary for your own healing—but you might have to take new actions. If you address your conflict and never get a good response, if you've tried many times and they never apologize or even seem to care that you're in pain, it's time for some hard decisions. You can read part 3, "How to Save Your Marriage by Yourself," for more details on what to do here. Or you can seek outside help. But apathy is something that should not go unchecked forever.

The timeline for trying before you leave is up to you. (Unless you're experiencing one of the four A's. Then it's time to get help.) It's great to go first and move through head, hands, heart, and habit. It's great to give your partner time. But you can't do this alone forever.

BOUNDARIES WITHIN FORGIVENESS

Once you've made forgiveness a habit, you can institute some boundaries to protect yourself from repetitive toxic behavior. This is how we make sure we're not condoning and tolerating the behavior that hurts us. Let's say your spouse tends to gossip about your family and it hurts you a lot. It's not good, healthy, or constructive. It's not working for your marriage, and it's causing you a significant amount of pain. And let's say you're living in forgiveness. You understand why they do that and have chosen to love them through it and not let the pain affect your decisions. You've asked them to stop doing it, and yet they haven't stopped. So what do you do?

You set a boundary. The next time they start gossiping about your family, you stop them right in their tracks and say, "I've asked you not to do that, and I won't tolerate it." Then you institute a consequence. Maybe you walk out of the room and resume talking only when they've agreed not to be mean about your family. Maybe you decide they're not invited to family functions anymore because you're uncomfortable knowing what they'll say later. You let them know they've crossed a boundary and you change *your* behavior. Walk away, stop talking, uninvite, etc. That is a good time to do one of the activities we mentioned in the Habit 7 chapter.

You have now set the expectation that you will no longer tolerate that behavior. Remember, we teach people how to treat us, and so far, you have let your spouse treat you that way (excluding domestic abuse here). Now it's time to forgive and set some healthy boundaries to protect yourself and your marriage. A helpful thing here is to keep reminding each other that you're a team. You're both on the side of the marriage. The whole reason you're engaging in this forgiveness process and boundary setting is because you love each other and want to stop hurting each other.

When you're sick and tired of pain that's turning you into

something you don't want to be, it's time to say, "Enough is enough." That's when you forgive, whether or not it comes naturally for you. It's definitely easier for some than others. Casey is much quicker to forgive than Meygan.

CASEY'S COACHING CORNER

I've found that seven out of ten times, men tend to be quicker to forgive. Maybe it's a guy thing or maybe men just make more mistakes than women (lol). But I think it's important to know that there are some people to whom forgiveness comes more naturally. If that's you, this is a superpower you have—a gift you should be grateful for!

There are no shortcuts to letting go. There is no replacement for the work of laying down a grudge and choosing peace over pride. But we promise, you can do it. Release the weight you've been holding on to and move forward lighter and stronger.

CONNECTING QUESTIONS

1. What are some challenges you face when trying to forgive me or others?

2. What do you need from me when you're struggling to forgive?

3. How can we create an environment where it's easier to ask for and offer forgiveness?

4. What's one thing I can do to make it easier for you to forgive me when I hurt you?

5. Are you usually quick to forgive or do you struggle to let go of the hurt? Have you always been this way and why?

The Sex Talk

Great sex starts with great conversations.

●————————————————————————————●

Well, folks, here we are. You've made it to the sex chapter. Or maybe you skipped right to it, you naughty little reader. If you did skip the rest of the book, here's a big ole spoiler for you: The best thing you can do for your sex life is to practice the first nine habits. Seriously. We even considered ending the chapter right there.

Habit 10: SEX
Do the other nine chapters' habits.
Then have sex and see the difference.
The end.

But we figured we'd give you a little more than that. So much of sex is about managing expectations. You have them, whether you know it consciously or not. We certainly did. Way back when, after we got home from our honeymoon, we sat in our living room and had our first naked dinner. "Why?" you might be asking. "Why in the world would you eat dinner naked?" That's a good question. The answer is: We honestly thought that all married couples ate dinner in the nude sometimes. We guess it came from some kind of Hollywood rom-com happily-ever-after, never-fall-out-of-love fairy-tale idea about what married couples did. Once we were married, we figured we'd do lots of normal activities while naked because . . . we don't know . . . that's just what married people do? What can we say, we were young and naïve and inexperienced and basically living in a fantasyland. Having dinner in the buff seemed fun and sexy. (And yes, we did cook the dinner fully clothed. We weren't *that* naïve.)

We made dinner, lit candles, set the table with our nice plates, poured some drinks, and even picked a Norah Jones playlist to set the mood. Then, we stripped down. Honestly, it was exactly how you're picturing it right now—pretty awkward. It's hard to eat naked and feel sexy. And of course, we desperately wanted to look sexy for each other. We felt vulnerable, and while it was a little exciting, we also later admitted to each other that we were wondering why the heck this seemed like a good idea. *Do married couples really do this a lot?*

As we sat there in the buff, we heard a quick knock on the front door and saw the knob start turning. For a split second, Casey thought it was a burglar and jumped up to defend his new bride. But then he quickly realized that a burglar probably wouldn't knock. He jumped over the table to block the door from opening, while Meygan streaked back to the bedroom, heart pounding.

Turns out, it was our friends from Sweden, bringing us wedding gifts but lacking the wisdom to call ahead and let us know they'd be stopping by. We put on some clothes and welcomed them into our home, flustered and embarrassed. To this day, we're still not sure what they think was going on in there and hope they didn't see anything. It's not like we've ever brought it up again.

The point is this: We had expectations! Whether you were aware of it or not, you got married and had expectations of what was "supposed" to happen in your sex life. They probably came from the same places our marriage assumptions came from. We develop these expectations by watching movies, listening to music, and having conversations with friends about sex. And that's normal and unavoidable. We are all the sum of our influences. The problem comes when we don't talk about our expectations, especially regarding sex.

The danger in expectations is this: If they are unrealistic, not communicated, or go unmet, we are left feeling disappointed, rejected, and alone. As psychotherapist and author Vanessa Marin says, "Sex is an incredibly intimate act, and not even acknowledging its existence can feel jarring."

Be honest: How often do you and your spouse talk about your sex life? And what do you talk about? Do you have any idea what each of your assumptions are?

SEX VS. INTIMACY

Let's zoom out for just a minute. Somewhere along the way, most of us started using *intimacy* and *sex* as interchangeable words. Many people believe they are one and the same. Though intimacy may include a physical act, there is much more to it than just sex. Intimacy encompasses an entire way of being, acting, and thinking. It is a place of commitment, vulnerability, interdependence, and trust. Intimacy is when both spouses understand each other and feel safe emotionally. It's what we've been building in the previous nine habits. That's why, by the time we start to talk about sex with our coaching clients, if they've been implementing the other tools, it's likely that their sex life has already vastly improved. They don't need too many of our little tips and tricks (though we certainly have them). Their sex life has already become what it's meant to be: a physical expression of their emotional intimacy.

Emotional intimacy in a marriage goes way beyond physical connection. An emotionally connected couple can share their feelings and thoughts freely, knowing they won't be judged or ignored. Intimacy is trusting your spouse to know you and not betray your vulnerabilities, especially during sex. And that intimacy is created, first and foremost, outside of the bedroom.

Here's how the other nine habits work to build the emotional bonds we're talking about:

Habit 1: The KNOWN Position

It teaches us to look at each other, touch each other, and see each other on a routine basis. Not just at night, and not just when it comes to sex.

Habit 2: The Weekly Marriage Business Meeting

Aligning with your spouse on time and responsibilities is a great way to build trust and intimacy. You can make sure you're each a priority to the other and show appreciation for everything you do. And remember, you schedule sex here. Get excited.

Habit 3: Love Lists

Is there anything else that builds emotional intimacy like showing you love each other in exactly the ways you each want to be loved? There's not much better foreplay than this.

Habit 4: The 60-Second Blessing

Few things help us get in the mood like showering each other with compliments. You've built each other up. Covered each other in love. And you can even turn this into a Sexy 60-Second Blessing to turn up the heat further. Details on that later.

Habit 5: Connection Time

You're laughing and encouraging each other, which is a great connection builder. It's hard to have a fun sex life if you don't have fun outside of the bedroom. This is why scheduled weekly connection time is such a nonnegotiable. And hopefully, you've been dreaming together too.

Habit 6: Leverage Your Differences

You know each other's strengths, weaknesses, and rhythms better than anyone else. If you've gotten into the habit of thinking more about your partner's positive qualities than their bad ones, this will translate into physical connection.

Habit 7: The Code Word

You've programmed yourselves to see conflict as an opportunity. When it comes up, you use it to learn how to love each other better. Now you can go into the bedroom with more safety and security because your arguments stay healthy.

Habit 8: Unsolicited Apologies

Almost nothing is more vulnerable than keeping short accounts and being quick to admit when you're wrong and ask for forgiveness. And vulnerability is emotionally connecting.

Habit 9: Head. Hands. Heart. Habit.

Why is make-up sex such a thing? Because forgiveness creates intimacy. Repairing a rupture makes you stronger than before. And often horny.

See? If you've been using the habits in this book, you've probably already created the emotional intimacy that will lead to having more physical intimacy. If you've nailed the other habits, you'll go into the bedroom with more safety and excitement than the couple who focus only on the actual sex. Sex without intimacy can be boring and leave you feeling like it was an obligation. Nobody wants that.

So, what's the best way to translate all this newfound emotional intimacy into great sex? Just have it! (Kidding.) First you need to *talk* about it. (Seriously, though. After talking, you do need to have it.) We're going to cover the four topics couples need to address when they talk about their sex lives. All your expectations and assumptions need to be aired, just like they do in every other area of your marriage. This should also be an ongoing conversation. If that just made you squirm, don't worry, you're not alone. If this isn't a regular habit for you, that's okay. For many people, it's not. But it should be. Dipping your toe into these topics is the single best way to prioritize your sex life.

MEYGAN'S INSIGHT

We highly recommend you have these conversations in the KNOWN position. Talking about sex is very vulnerable, and you need to communicate clearly about it with your partner.

THE CONVERSATIONS

Set aside time, maybe during connection time or a date night, to try out one of these four conversation starters.

Foreplay

Conversation starter: What turns you on the most outside of the bedroom? What kind of foreplay do you like and why?

Foreplay isn't just about getting in the mood. It's about connection, anticipation, and mutual satisfaction. It's way, way more than just a quick bedroom warm-up. For many couples, especially women, foreplay is crucial for both physical and emotional readiness. Women's bodies operate more like slow cookers, while men's are more like microwaves. It's just a biological difference that means women often need more runway. You can't wait until five minutes before the act to woo her.

As we said, this all starts outside the bedroom. You can even think about the other habits as foreplay. Or even pre-foreplay. Flirting, touching, and verbal affirmation throughout the day can build anticipation. And though this is extra important for women, men certainly benefit from extended arousal too. Share your feelings, express gratitude, and show affection—every day, but especially on the day that sex is on your calendar. Think of your words and actions as foreplay. Help with the dishes, send a thoughtful text, or compliment your spouse on something they accomplished at work. Pick an item or two off their Love List and do it on the day leading up to sex.

Of course, foreplay is a fun and helpful part of intercourse as well. We 100 percent encourage things like oral sex, hand jobs, intimate touching, making out, massage, and vibrators, though we won't get into details here in this book. (We have tons of sexy tips and techniques on our website. We also have a worksheet with a foreplay inventory to help you figure out what you like so you can communicate it to your partner. You can download that at Marriage365Books.com/resources.)

When we tell couples to communicate openly, honestly, and without shame about what they enjoy sexually, many people respond with "I'm not even sure what I like." If that's you, download our app to walk through some questions and exercises that will help you in that self-discovery. Once you know what you like and what gets you in the mood, you can create a Sexy Love List. It's exactly like the original Love List from habit 3, but spicy. You can mention traits you like about your spouse's body, or bedroom activities they do that you enjoy. Compliment them in sexy ways and about the sex you have together.

MEYGAN'S INSIGHT

Foreplay is a broad term. Women say they want it, and husbands don't know what they mean. So the more specific you can be, the better.

Frequency

Conversation starter: How do you feel about scheduling sex versus letting it happen spontaneously?

Are you surprised to know that one of the most asked questions we get, out of the hundreds of topics we speak on regularly, is "How often should we be having sex?" What's often encoded in that is "Are we normal?" and "Are we having it enough?" and "What does it say about us?" It's loaded, right? And ripe for comparison if you find out someone else is having sex more often.

When we first got married, we thought we'd be going at it like rabbits all the time. Reality hit quickly when we realized life gets in the way. The mundanity sets in: bills, chores, kids. Or maybe there's a big life event that affects how often you have sex. Maybe you lose your job or a family member gets a devastating diagnosis. For all those reasons, it can be counterproductive to judge our sex lives by the frequency rather than the quality.

The short answer to our most asked question is that there's no "normal" frequency. What matters is that both partners feel satisfied and connected. If you really want to go by the data, the average married couple has sex about once a week. That's not right for everyone, but if you're looking for a benchmark to start with, that's what we suggest. Schedule it once a week during your WMBM. And if it happens more, great! If you are having spontaneous sex and you're both satisfied with the quality and quantity, you could skip to the next section. If you discover that once a week is a little too much for you right now, and you need to scale back to once every other, or once a month, that's also fine, as long as you come to that conclusion together and you're both satisfied with the quality of your sex.

As we wrote earlier, one of the biggest pushbacks we get when we talk about scheduling sex is that people are worried it won't be exciting or satisfying anymore. (Which is ironic, because not having it at all is the *actual* least exciting and least satisfying option, and that's often the current situation.) Most of the movies we watch and books we read depict sex as something that just happens without thought or planning. But real life doesn't work that way. We plan for work projects, oil changes, school projects, haircuts, doctor appointments, and even what we eat for dinner, yet we expect sex to be spontaneous.

Your sex life may not be as spontaneous as what we see in movies, but that doesn't mean it cannot be as fulfilling or exciting. In popular culture, sex sells, but only a particular type of sex. The spontaneous, apropos of nothing, "push you up against the wall unexpectedly" kind of sex is what we're presented with. Sex that is routine and ordinary doesn't come up as much. It's not as cinematic or dramatic. And that's the problem with this expectation. We go into relationships and *expect* it to be spontaneous and not routine and ordinary. Throw two full-time jobs, a couple of kids, a dog, a house, and hobbies into the mix, and that spontaneity is just not realistic during many seasons. Or ever. If we're conditioning ourselves to expect something different, of course we'll end up disappointed, frustrated, and angry.

There are plenty of seasons and life circumstances that will affect the frequency of sex. Here are just a few:

- Young kids
- Pregnancy
- Medications
- Travel
- Military work
- Shift work

- Full-time work for both parents
- Stress (the number one cause of libido drop, in our opinion)
- Health issues

So, we'll say it again: Schedule it. If you don't believe us and think that it won't be fun or satisfying, fine. Put it to the test. Try it just for a few weeks. Write "Have sex" at nine o'clock on Wednesday nights and see what happens when you notice that scheduled event every time you open your calendar app. Come back and tell us with a straight face that you don't get a little excited when you see it. That knowing it's coming doesn't help you get prepared. That you're not extra loving and attentive on Wednesday morning. That you don't feel that twinge of anticipation or start getting ideas about how to make Wednesday evening a little more special. Not a single person out of all the thousands that we've ever worked with has come back and said, "Boy, I sure did hate scheduling sex and was so bummed that we both orgasmed." Be so for real. This just plain works.

CASEY'S COACHING CORNER

During the seasons of life when it feels right, we like to aim for one quick, often spontaneous sex sesh, and one longer and intentional one per week. Because spontaneous sex can be great. We highly encourage it. It's only when it becomes an unmet expectation that it's a problem.

Feelings

Conversation starter: What are some things we can do that will create a safe environment for us to have constructive and healthy conversations about sex?

Since sex isn't just a physical act, so much of what stops us from having it in a satisfying way isn't physical. It's emotional. It's our feelings.

Meygan remembers a time when she felt disconnected from Casey emotionally. Even though we were still having sex, it felt hollow and unsatisfying. She hated that feeling. It took some honest conversations and vulnerability to realize that our emotional intimacy needed work. Once we addressed those issues, our physical intimacy improved dramatically.

This is a huge part of what we mean by talking about your sex life. Yes, you can mention to your spouse that you liked that thing they did with their tongue the other night, but we also mean saying things like "I feel anxious about my body since I just had a baby." Here are some more real-life examples of feelings we've heard couples express around sex:

- I'm feeling confused about why we used to have sex often and now it seems sporadic.

- I feel like we're lacking emotional connection, and because of that, it's impacting my libido.

- I'm recognizing that my past sexual trauma from my childhood is impacting the way I'm showing up in the bedroom.

- I feel excited that we're empty nesters and now get to have more opportunities to have fun sexually.

- I've felt for some time that we've been struggling to be open and vulnerable in our daily conversations, and it's making me have a wall up in the bedroom.

- I'm feeling hopeful that we're at a better place emotionally and sexually than we were last year at this time.

- I've been feeling a little weird as I'm the one who's been initiating sex lately.

- I'm really satisfied with where our sex life is in this season.

- I've been struggling to relax during sex knowing that our kids' bedrooms are right around the corner. I worry they may hear us.

How about you? What would you say if your partner asked you to sum up your feelings toward sex?

It's important to regularly check in with each other, not just about the act of sex itself but about your feelings around it. Discuss any fears or insecurities openly. This might be a place where one or both of you need to offer a four-step apology if mistakes have been made. Maybe you've cared more about physical intimacy than emotional intimacy. Maybe you've attempted sex with your partner at an insensitive time or withheld it as a form of punishment. Maybe you've even tried something in the bedroom that they didn't like and you need to make that right. Practice spousal awareness. Understand how your partner's day-to-day experiences affect their desire levels. This is an ongoing and fluid conversation. As your lives and relationship ebb and flow, so will your feelings about sex. Don't put so much pressure on yourself to feel the same way about it all the time. And don't expect your partner to be able to tell how you're feeling without you explicitly saying it.

Yes, all of this is incredibly vulnerable. But if you've built that emotional intimacy, telling your partner that you're insecure about your body or working through some trauma will give them a chance to understand you better and support you. And explicitly stating how great sex has been and how excited you are about it will only encourage more of it. You can go to

Marriage365Books.com/resources for even more connecting questions specifically aimed to help you each clarify your feelings about sex at this point in your life.

Fun

Conversation starter: What's a fun way we could surprise each other in the bedroom?

Sex should be fun. Do we even need to say that? Most people are quick to agree that sex is enjoyable. But too often couples get stuck in a rut and forget to have fun in the bedroom. They forget to be playful, not take it too seriously, and try new things at the risk of getting it "wrong." Sex certainly doesn't have to be serious or perfect. In fact, it shouldn't be. That's just too much pressure. If sex is a reflection of the rest of your relationship, you should relax, laugh, and experiment. Here are some ways to inject more fun into your intimate moments:

- Try new things together. New positions, locations, or sensory experiences can be fun. You can find a long list at Marriage365Books.com/resources.

- Don't be afraid to laugh. Sex can be awkward, and that's okay! Embrace the funny moments. We promise, it won't kill the mood. Laugh and keep right on going.

- Create a sexy playlist. Music can set the mood and help you both relax. One night we were having sex to a live Dave Matthews concert soundtrack and happened to "finish" right as the audience applauded. It was perfect, and hilarious.

- Play bedroom games. There are plenty of adult games designed to spice things up.

Remember, the goal is to connect and enjoy each other. Don't put too much pressure on performance or perfection. Like everything in marriage, be humble and experiment. Try new things and be curious about each other.

To really kick things up a notch, especially on days when you're looking forward to sex, try a Sexy 60-Second Blessing. Spend sixty seconds showering each other with affection and appreciation, like you would in a normal 60-Second Blessing—but this time, make it sexy. List body parts you like, how your spouse turns you on, things they do that get you going, etc. It's just an R-rated version. In our opinion, this is some of the best foreplay.

•————————————————•

CONNECTING QUESTIONS

1. Which of the four F's (foreplay, frequency, feelings, and fun) do you think we should focus on and why?

2. What are some ways we can increase our emotional intimacy outside of the bedroom?

3. Are there any new things you'd like to try when it comes to foreplay?

4. What's one way we can make sex feel more exciting and fun?

5. What are some ways we can make scheduled sex feel spontaneous and fun?

PART III

How to Save Your Marriage by Yourself

Many people look at us as an example of a happy, healthy marriage. And we're honored by that. Gratefully, we are happy and healthy—now. But as you know from hearing our story throughout this book, we certainly weren't always that way. The first few years were bad. Really, really bad.

We needed help, and while we were both unhappy and recognized this couldn't go on, we weren't on the same page about how to fix it. Casey was closed off and not ready to get outside help. But I (Meygan) desperately wanted that help. Not because I'm better or more honorable or anything like that. I was just more predisposed to taking action and seeking help because of my personality and upbringing. In marriage, things are rarely fifty-fifty. Someone almost always has to go first and care more. At least for a while. When it came to saving our marriage, that person was going to have to be me.

Based on statistics and anecdotal data from our Marriage365 app, more than half of you reading this aren't reading it with your spouse. You're reading it alone, hoping you can evoke a change in your marriage. If that's you, know that you can. I'm proof of that. But it didn't start with me changing Casey. Well, to be honest, I did *try* to start it that way. On that first day of therapy, I came prepped with everything he was doing wrong and every way I wished he was different. I sat on a couch with a therapist I had never met before and talked about how bad my husband was. "Yeah, sure, I have some problems too. But really, when it comes down to it, our marriage is in this bad place because of *him*. He doesn't want to get help, he doesn't forgive, he doesn't apologize, we don't have fun anymore . . ." On and on I went. I was fired up, even energized by finally letting out all the hatred and anger and frustration and sadness I'd felt over the years.

She sat there and listened. She scribbled on her notepad as I talked. Then, when I'd finally calmed down and taken a breath, she looked up at me and said, "But he's not here. You are. So I'd like to see you again next week, and I'm going to give you two options. I'll respect whichever one you choose. Option one, you come back next week and share what's going on in your life, like you did today. I can validate you. I can listen to you. We can work through some unprocessed trauma from childhood, and I'll just be that safe person for you to talk to. I'm that to many of my clients." That sounded nice. I'd never had anyone in my life like that before. "Okay," I said. "What's option two?"

"Option two is this: I can teach you how to be a healthy spouse. Meygan, I can show you how to communicate to bring defenses down and feel confident in your words. I can teach you how to implement and follow through with boundaries so your husband learns he can't treat you that way anymore. I can show you how to forgive him and ask him to forgive you and how to let it go, no matter if he's sorry or not. You'll become not just a healthy spouse but a healthy person. I don't know if we can heal your marriage, but I know we can work on healing you so no matter what, whether you stay or go, you're content with who you are and how you showed up. If your marriage ends, I want you to be able to answer this question: Have I done everything and anything I possibly could to save my marriage so that I won't live with regret?"

It was like a dagger to the heart. I knew my answer, at that moment, was no. I hadn't done everything I could to save my marriage. I hadn't really tried. I'd read books, complained to my friends, tried a technique here and there, and argued with Casey, and then I'd gotten frustrated and checked out. I knew I had to pick option two. I had to at least try and give it my all. It felt like a Hail Mary, but my therapist was right. I'd regret it for the rest of my life if I didn't try. I had to be able to live with myself, to look in the mirror every morning and be proud of who I was. At that moment, I wasn't especially proud of who I was. I knew I was miserable and started fights and nagged and complained constantly. I didn't want to be that person, with or without Casey. So, over the next thirteen months, I worked on changing how I showed up—both inside and outside of our marriage.

In this chapter I'm going to detail the seven steps I took to save my marriage by myself. Right up front, I want to address something that you might be thinking, because I certainly was back then. *Why does it have to be me? Why do I have to go first? Why can't he get better? Why do I have to be the bigger and better person? This isn't fair.* (Quick reminder: This doesn't have to do with the four A's. If you're experiencing any of those, your job is not to be the bigger person. It's to get out safely and get help.)

I understand. I *love* things to be fair. You probably figured that out about me by now. Hearing that I was going to have to do all the work while he didn't do any (at least at first) was a hard hurdle to get over. Let me validate that feeling for you: It does suck. It's not fun. It'd be much easier if your spouse was on board right away. But they aren't. And this kind of work is worth it. Not just for your marriage, but for you. And if you have kids, certainly for them too. If you're so bitter you can hardly see straight, it can help to think of your work that way—as something you're doing for you, not for your spouse. I promise, it's worth it.

STEP 1:
BE ALL IN

All right, step number one is to be all in.

Working on your marriage without a willing spouse might feel like a part-time job. You'll have to make time to go to therapy, journal, cry, process feelings, get comfortable exploring your emotions, meet with a safe friend, and ask yourself really tough questions. There is a lot of work coming your way. Good, worthwhile stuff. But work, nonetheless. And at some point, you're going to feel like giving up. I guarantee there will be days when you'll think this is too much. *I'm doing all the work and my spouse is doing nothing.* But you'll regret it if you give up too early. This isn't a quick-fix "do these steps, answer a couple of journal questions, and everything will be hunky-dory" solution. This is a process. It's ugly and messy sometimes. But at the end, there's peace and freedom.

I encourage you to put visual reminders all over your desk or wherever you'll see them. I put some in my notebooks, by my nightstand, in my car, in the books I was reading. I wrote the exact phrase that we use at Marriage365 today: *If you want to make a better marriage, make a better you.* You can use whatever quote or saying helps you remember that you're not giving up. You have control over you. You can't control your spouse. Remind yourself that you're improving your own life. I even put up a few connecting questions that really inspired me in that season. Put them everywhere so you'll never forget what the end goal is. *I get to be healthy. I get to answer yes to that question—I did everything and anything I could to save my marriage.*

STEP 2:
GET OUTSIDE HELP AND SUPPORT

The reality is that most of us need accountability. I certainly did in that season. I needed someone to tell me, in a firm but loving way, what I was doing wrong and where I could improve. Find a safe friend like my therapist mentioned. Maybe it's a mentor or a therapist. Maybe you also speak to a pastor. Whoever it is, you need someone in your life who is not going to judge you. They will support you in this season.

We weren't meant to do life alone. We need someone who can meet us right where we are, not where we think we should be. You need at least one safe person you can say anything to, who you know is on your team. This will not be a person who tells you to get divorced immediately or thinks you're crazy or stupid. It also will not be someone who is prone to gossip. You might even want to get rid of those people for a while, no matter how close you are to them. You can say something as simple as "Right now, I'm going through a lot in my life, and I need to do my own thing, so please just be patient with me. I'll reach out in a few months." Your request for space doesn't mean they're a horrible person; it just means they don't need to be a part of this journey with you. The only people invited into what you're doing should be people who will love and support you while challenging you to be that healthy spouse. Consider a temporary life audit to ensure you're surrounded by as much love and support as you can get.

At the beginning of this book, you heard us say that many couples don't need more therapy; they need better tools. And we deeply believe that. But if you're trying to save your marriage by yourself, a therapist or life coach is a great idea. There is no shame in saying, "I don't think I can do this on my own." On those days when you feel like giving up, the safe person you've chosen is the one you can call or text. When you say, "I'm struggling," they'll remind you that you're doing the right thing.

STEP 3:
PREPARE YOURSELF FOR AN UNHEALTHY RESPONSE

I can promise you that as you do this work, your spouse is going to get mad, yell at you, mock you, give you the silent treatment, ignore you, or tease you for getting help and healing. You know why? Because they aren't healthy yet. If they were, you wouldn't be on this journey in the first place. They would already be doing the work alongside you. Even though they likely also realize things are bad, they're not going to like that you've gone ahead and changed something. Unhealthy people respond in unhealthy ways, especially when they're confronted with new, healthy behaviors. It's going to shine a spotlight on their struggles, which won't feel good.

So, I don't want you to go into this thinking that your spouse will notice the change immediately, affirm you, and fix themselves. It might happen. But probably not. Like any purge, things might get worse before they get better.

But I also don't want you to worry about that response. It's a knee-jerk reaction. You've both developed an unhealthy pattern, and now you're bucking it. If you can, try not to worry about what your spouse thinks about you. I know that is much easier said than done. You love them. And once upon a time, if not still, you cared more about what they thought than anyone else in the world. This gets easier as the months go on. As you become confident and healthier, their response won't trigger you anymore. Stay the course.

STEP 4:
COMMIT TO BECOMING SELF-AWARE AND CONFIDENT

In this season, you'll be learning a lot about yourself. It's almost like you're studying to write a textbook about you. I want you to get to know your strengths, talents, triggers, fears, and struggles. How do you respond to conflict and life's challenges? How do the people in your life perceive you? What do they say about you? How did they experience you? Look at your childhood—the good, the bad, and the ugly. What have you processed? What have you not processed? What are your core beliefs? What are your values? What are the things that drive you crazy?

When you make time for your emotional health, you will naturally become more self-aware. And self-aware people have confidence. You will know your worth. You will know your value. You'll work on your insecurities because you know who you are.

At first, this will be really hard. All of us have negative traits and patterns that we need to confront. I'm sure right now there are plenty of things you don't like about yourself that you could name right off the bat. But as you look behind the curtain, focus on the good parts of you, and grow in your struggles, you'll become much more balanced. You'll know where you're strong and where you're weak, and you'll appreciate those things about yourself. Confidence comes from this kind of self-awareness. Insecurities can be loud, but confidence is quiet (and sexy). And when you find confidence in this way, it enables you to act with calm security the next time your spouse does or says something that used to bug you (and maybe still does). You don't have to make a remark back to them. It's not worth spending your time on. It's not who you want to be. It's beneath you.

The connecting questions at the end of this chapter will be a great guide to help you start your self-discovery process. We even have a whole book, *365 Self Discovery Questions*, that you can use if you want more. The questions can be used as journal prompts. Just choose one a day and journal it out. You'll learn a lot about yourself.

Of course, if you go to therapy, or if you work with a coach online or in person, you'll have someone to guide you in this process. But even if you don't, you can journal your way to getting to know yourself and getting your confidence back.

STEP 5:
START GIVING UNSOLICITED APOLOGIES

If you read the apology chapter, you might have seen this coming. Remember, apologies are what we do for others when we recognize that we've hurt them and we want to make things better.

Apologizing is a sign of maturity and growth. People who blame others are typically insecure, prideful, and hurting. A huge step in this journey of healing your marriage is to begin owning your stuff—and saying it out loud to your spouse. This means getting rid of your pride. No more blaming.

I was extremely guilty of this in my marriage. I was a blamer. I thought most things were Casey's fault.

I learned not only that I was guilty of getting plenty of things wrong but also that admitting to them had a way of bringing Casey's defenses down. When you look hard at your faults and face them in the mirror, it takes away their power. You don't have to shift blame or make excuses or have an explanation. You just have to say, "Yes, that was my fault. I'm sorry." It's so freeing. Your mistakes don't have power anymore. Instead, *you* have the power.

So, here's what you're going to do. Write down at least ten things you can apologize for. Honestly, when I did this, I realized my list was almost fifty strong. I needed to apologize to Casey for many things, big and small. Here are just a few:

- Being a nag
- Not initiating sex
- Giving him the silent treatment
- Trying to control him
- Trying to change him
- Being brutally honest
- Not being a great communicator
- Not validating his feelings
- Being a fixer
- Threatening divorce too many times to count

What this looked like in practice was me randomly going up to him and offering an unsolicited apology for something on the list every few days. This will catch your spouse off guard—which, if you're like most hurting couples, breaks a deep pattern. You're not telling them that they're wrong, which is what the old you would have done. You're humbly saying, "I am so sorry. I want to make things better." It shows your spouse that you care about their feelings. Remember, their response isn't what matters here. They may respond in an unhealthy way at first. You won't know until you try. But don't apologize hoping they will say, "Wow, thank you so much. Your healthiness has motivated me to offer you my own apology." Nope. That's unlikely to happen the first time. Or even the tenth. But of course, if it does, fantastic.

One of my first apologies to Casey was about failing to show empathy toward him. He had so many struggles in those early years of marriage: finding and keeping jobs, dealing with an un-predictable extended family, coping with ADHD, and generally learning how to be an adult without any guidance. He had com-plained many, many times that I was not empathetic and didn't validate his feelings. So one day, when we were both calm and not distracted—the TV wasn't on, and we weren't running off somewhere—I approached him and said, "I wanted to say some-thing to you. I recognize that I struggle with empathy, and I know you've shared that with me. I know you feel like I don't listen to you, like I don't validate you and I just want to fix you. I want to say: You're right. I'm not a great listener, and it's something I really need to work on. When I don't validate you, you probably feel very unseen, disrespected, unheard, and alone in our marriage. You don't deserve that. I was wrong. If there's anything I can do to make this better, I hope you'll share it with me. And I hope one day you can forgive me."

He. Was. Shocked. So shocked that he didn't really say much. But I knew my words landed because his jaw dropped almost to the floor.

A few days would go by, and I'd return to the list and pick something else. I offered him another four-step apology about being a nag and asked for his forgiveness. No matter your part-ner's response, that's what you do. One thing after another. Own your stuff, and don't worry about the outcome. I'm telling you, it might be counterintuitive and hard to start, but once you get going, this feels great. Release your mistakes. Admit you're imperfect. Your spouse will see that, and ideally this behavior will rub off on them and they'll start apologizing too. But the point is that *you'll* feel better. You'll feel lighter and healthier. So make that list of at least ten things, and one by one, apologize for them every few days. As you continue making mistakes in your marriage, continue to apologize. Be the fastest and the first, because that's what emotionally healthy spouses and people do.

STEP 6:
FORGIVE THEM

This is the hardest step for most people. It was for me. Your spouse might not be sorry. They probably aren't asking for forgiveness. They're not changing, they're not working on themselves, and they're certainly not grateful for all the work you're doing. Yet . . . you need to forgive them. Forgiveness is a choice, not a feeling. It's a choice you make to let them off the hook for the pain they've caused you, whether they knew they were causing you pain or not.

When my therapist first told me I needed to work on forgiving Casey, I said, "But how do you forgive someone you hate?" Ouch, I know. But maybe you can relate. Have you ever felt like you hated your spouse? Or at least you thought you didn't like them very much? How do you forgive someone who's not really sorry and whom you can't stand most days? There are three techniques that helped me a lot, in addition to the four H's that we covered in habit 9.

Remember, to forgive someone, you start by seeing them with compassion. Get curious about why your spouse is in pain. There's something magical about jumping into the driver's seat of your spouse's car and trying to see life the way they see it. What's their perspective? What are all the things that happened in their life that led them to this place of hurt?

Here are a few things I noticed about Casey. He had a traumatic childhood, though he never would've said he did. When I met him, he normalized it. And when we got married, it was evident to me that he never really processed it. That was a big aha moment for me. When I envisioned him as a little boy and imagined all the broken homes he'd lived in and blended families he'd been a part of, I had so much compassion and understanding for why he was the way he was.

I wanted Casey to be a healthy husband, but he had no idea how to do that. He didn't have anybody in his life who modeled what a healthy marriage could look like. He never learned how to communicate or talk about sex and boundaries. He was raised in a home where, no matter how bad things got, you did *not* go to therapy. I don't think anybody in his family has ever seen a therapist. I was raised entirely differently. My parents didn't have a great marriage, but I grew up watching them go to therapy. And then when they divorced, they forced me to go. I'm so glad they did. Getting help was a more normal attitude, which is why it was easier for me to go first in our marriage.

Gaining this spousal awareness was such a lightbulb experience for me. No wonder Casey didn't want to go to therapy, despite my begging. That doesn't mean he was right, but the explanation behind his behavior helped me forgive—and decide what to do next.

The second thing that helps when forgiving your spouse is to write them a letter about all the ways they've hurt you. Don't hold back, because they're not going to read it. Don't worry about penmanship or grammar or length. Then, when you're done, when you feel like you've written everything you possibly can about all the pain they've brought into your life, burn it. Turn on your fireplace and toss it in.

There's something therapeutic about that visual—seeing your words of pain and anguish burning up in the ashes. Those experiences, the hurtful comments, the laziness, the neglect, the abandonment, the cusswords . . . they're gone. The fire has burned them up. They're done, and you are no longer going to hold on to that. You've literally and figuratively let it go.

Last, we're going to trick your brain again. Therapists probably have better terminology than that, but it's how I think of this third technique. Remember how we said our brains love to focus on the negative, but we're going to rewire them for positive? Next time you start to feel triggered or angry—when your resentment builds up again and you can feel it about to boil over—immediately stop what you're doing and take out a piece of paper. It doesn't matter if you're driving, at the office, or with the kids. Stop in your tracks, take out some paper (or your note-taking app on your phone), and write five to ten true, positive things that you appreciate about your spouse.

In moments like these, your brain is fixated on the negative. If you continue down that line of thinking, you're going to hate who you become as you lean even further into unforgiving. So hit the brakes. I used to do this exercise all the time. I even kept an early list I made on a piece of paper. It's pretty ragged. It's in my journal from April 2006. Here's what it says:

- Casey is a hard worker.
- He's funny.
- He took out the trash yesterday.
- He still thinks I'm sexy.
- God loves him.
- He's hurting. He's insecure. That's why he's hurting me.
- He called my insurance company to figure out my prescription issue.

I know it's random, but that's the point. You're tricking your brain at that moment to say, *I'm no longer going to give life to these toxic and unhealthy thoughts. I'm going to move forward and choose to forgive now.*

I need you to know that it took me about six months to get to the place where I couldn't hold the unforgiveness anymore. Then, finally, I forgave him. It was excruciatingly hard. And there were still days when I wanted to go back to that resentment and frustration and allow myself to stew in unforgiveness. Because, let's be honest, it feels good for a while. It's justified, right?

Maybe it was, but the cost wasn't worth the temporary satisfaction. My bitterness was affecting my sleep, my conversations, my thoughts, my friendships, everything. I tried so hard to hold on to it. I sat on my therapist's chair and bad-mouthed Casey for forty-five minutes, and it felt righteous. But eventually, I got tired of it. Going through the four H's of forgiveness and making short lists of gratitude helped me release the resentment. And it brought me much more peace and satisfaction than rumination or self-righteousness ever did.

STEP 7:
SET CLEAR, HEALTHY BOUNDARIES

Just because you've forgiven your spouse doesn't mean they get to keep on hurting you, right? Remember, forgiveness does not mean we condone bad behavior. It's time for you to teach them how to treat you moving forward, because you are no longer going to tolerate unhealthy behavior.

Boundaries are about prioritizing and protecting your marriage. Now that you know your worth and know that you deserve love and respect (and so does your spouse, BTW), guess what? It's time to show the behaviors you'll no longer tolerate. Decide what behaviors are impacting you personally, causing major stress in your life. Maybe they're killing your confidence. Maybe they're making you feel overwhelmed or insecure. Whatever they are, write them down. We're going to set some boundaries around them.

I'll give you an example. You can steal it if you want. Casey used to cuss me out and call me names. People who know him now can hardly believe it, but it's true. (To be fair, Old Meygan would also cuss him out. We've both come a long way.) I wanted to change that pattern. We both deserved respect in our marriage. Our arguments could still get heated, but we needed to respect each other. I wasn't going to tolerate the yelling, the cussing, and the name-calling anymore. That was the boundary.

If we got into an argument and he started exhibiting those behaviors, I'd stand up and say, "I love you. We both deserve respect. I'm no longer going to tolerate you treating me like this. So when you're calm, I would love to talk to you about this." Then I'd walk away.

Casey loves to have the last word. He would say, "Oh, there you go, walking away again" or "Oh, there you go, giving up on our marriage" or "Oh, look at you, all fancy-pants with your therapeutic techniques." Remember, you can't control your partner's response. Don't listen to them. When you're confident and not expecting a certain response, you can move into boundaries in a healthy way. You respect yourself enough to say, "No one is allowed to cuss me out. No one's allowed to treat me this way." I did this for about four months, every single time things got ugly, until finally, Casey got the message and the cussing finally stopped.

Another boundary came when I noticed he was sharing about our marriage problems with people I considered unsafe. My boundary was that we'd share only with people whom both of us viewed as loving and supportive. So I said, "I know you're sharing with so-and-so, but if you continue to share with that person, I'm not going to be coming around parties or family gatherings when they're there. I won't tolerate that because I asked you not to share." For a little bit he actually did continue, and I had to enforce the boundary. We were invited to parties, and I didn't go. Again, boundaries are about teaching your spouse what behaviors are okay and what behaviors are unacceptable. While you cannot control what they decide to do, you can decide what you will and won't allow.

The webinar I teach on "How to Save Your Marriage Alone" is always in our top three most popular lessons. Much of what I learned along the way became the foundation of Marriage365 and our methods for helping couples and individuals today. Below are the answers to some of the most common questions I get asked from people going through this.

Did you have sex during this time?

We did, but to be honest, it wasn't great. It happened infrequently, and it wasn't very satisfying for me. But I knew that sex was very important for Casey to feel connected. He loves to express his love that way. Withholding it from him because he wouldn't go to therapy with me or because he wasn't as engaged in fixing our marriage felt like it would just make things worse. In general, things were always better between us when we were having sex. Our daily interactions might have been awkward, and there were plenty of days where we walked on eggshells around each other. We didn't talk about deep things, and our relationship felt very surface level. But sex (and our nightly card playing) was one place where we could still connect, even if it was far from perfect.

That being said, I never felt harmed or violated during sex in this season. You get to choose what your physical relationship looks like while you're healing your marriage on your own. If having sex feels like it will do more harm than good, for you or for both of you, abstaining might be better.

How vulnerable should I be with my spouse during this time?

I believe, with my whole heart, that you should be vulnerable only with the people who appreciate your vulnerability. If your spouse is closed off, hardened to you, and living in unforgiveness, being vulnerable with them is probably not a good idea. What's the point of you sharing? If you've tried being vulnerable already and they've responded negatively, would you be okay if that happened again? Because in all likelihood, it will. They won't appreciate or understand your vulnerability, so I'd be very careful with your heart during this season until things change.

How did you trust Casey?

In short, I didn't trust Casey during this season. We don't open our hearts to people we don't trust. We aren't vulnerable with people we don't trust. But at one point during this year of our marriage, I had an aha moment in counseling. I'd had a chaotic childhood, and often children who experience this grow up to be controlling because we're trying to ensure we don't experience chaos again. For the first time in a long time, I had the instinct to share those memories with Casey. So one day, when everything between us was "good" and calm, I said, "Hey, I just wanted to share with you about something that happened in my therapy session." And I told him about my revelation, which led to me apologizing because he'd been right about how much I'd tried to control him. That day, his response was fine. Probably because he was more shocked than anything else. But it was a good sign to me. *Okay, he can be kind when I approach certain issues. Maybe I'll try again soon.*

That's how I counsel people to try. Go in with zero expectations, when the emotional temperature is good, and see what happens. See if you can trust your partner with a little vulnerability. If they still decide to get defensive, lash out, or shut down, I wouldn't continue to share openly. Don't invite them into your deep, heartfelt thoughts, because they haven't earned that.

Over time, I did learn to trust Casey. I shared more of my thoughts and feelings, little by little, in calm moments. And when he reacted positively, or at least not negatively, it gave me courage to try again. Eventually, he started trying too.

How long will this take? How long am I really supposed to fight for my marriage by myself? When is enough enough?

The answer here might annoy you: It's different for everybody. But you guys should know by now that I'm all about the practical, helpful answers. My timeline was two years. I didn't share it with Casey, but in my own heart and mind, I said, *For two years I'm doing these seven steps and everything and anything I can to fix this marriage. I'm going to get healthy for two years, and if he doesn't notice, or if he's not willing to change, or if he hasn't made any kind of progress, I'm going to ask for a separation.*

I always advise people to rate how bad things are on a scale of one to ten (ten being really, really bad). Have you felt alone for years, maybe decades? Have you tried what feels like every action to get your spouse's attention, and you're still getting nothing from them? Has it been a long time since you felt like a team? Is there no communication, love, laughter, or emotional safety in your marriage? If yes, you're on the higher end of that scale. I rated my marriage an eight and a half during this time. The point of rating is to get honest with yourself about the state of things and about how long it might take to repair the marriage. If you're at a one, meaning it's not too bad and you can just sense that things are headed in the wrong direction, you might need only a couple of months, maybe weeks. But if you're closer to ten, you'll likely be on my timeline, which was years.

Remember the four A's (abuse, affairs, addiction, and abandonment). If any of the last three are present in your marriage, you should probably have a shorter timeline and not put up with that for as long. (And if there is any form of abuse, forget the scale. You need to separate and get help.) But in general, I tell people that outside of the four A's, you should do these seven steps for a minimum of six months before you throw in the towel. The average person needs about one to two years to feel like they've given this their all and done what they could.

Getting healthy requires a lot of work and effort. The most important thing is that, at the end of the day, at the end of this season, however long you've been in it, you can be proud of your answer to the question my therapist asked me: Have you done everything and anything you possibly could to save your marriage so that you won't live with regret? If your answer is yes after two years, but nothing is different, then separation is probably the next step. Or if you're already separated, maybe divorce. You can live with the confidence that you tried. You did your job, and you did it well.

This journey for me ended at thirteen months. Despite everything that had happened to our marriage, I was feeling great. I felt like a completely different person, and I was proud of myself. I'd come a long way with my boundaries and communication. And I knew what I deserved. I'd seen tiny changes in Casey in response to this, but nothing yet to suggest he was ready to make much effort. Until one Friday night, in our tiny, cramped apartment, we were getting into another one of those arguments we'd had a thousand times. Thirteen months earlier, I would have engaged in an unhealthy way. But this time, I didn't go there. I held my boundary again and said I wouldn't continue this fight with him if he was going to yell and shame me.

As I turned and started walking to another room, Casey dropped to his knees and said, "I give up." I spun around and looked at him. I wasn't sure what he meant. "Whatever you've done," he continued, "I want to do it too. I'm tired. I'm exhausted. I'm embarrassed. I don't want to live like this anymore. I'm jealous of you."

And so Casey began his own healing process. In the last year, he'd said hardly a word about my growth. There was too much pride. But this is what happens when you embark on the journey. There will be a point, whether they admit it or not, when your partner sees the changes you've made and notices the stark contrast between them and you. There will be nothing else to do but change, or it will be over. Those are the only options.

You can't be in a marriage with just one person. Eventually, if it's going to work, your spouse will have to come along. I don't know your story, and I don't know your dynamic. But what I do know is this: You have control over your words, your communication, your forgiveness, your apologies, your attitude, your behavior, your habits, and your life. You have zero control over your spouse. Do not wait for them to come on board. You will waste your time and build resentment. Do not let things get so bad that you don't even know who you are anymore when you look in the mirror.

Do I know whether you can save your marriage by yourself? No, I don't. But I know you can save *yourself*. I believe in you. And you have a whole community of people out there supporting you who are doing the same thing. You will be proud of yourself at the end of this journey, however long that is for you. We're in this together.

CONNECTING QUESTIONS

1. What would it take for you to make time to become more self-aware, heal, and grow emotionally? And what's currently standing in your way?

2. What are some of your thoughts, fears, and hesitations about paying little to no attention to your spouse's negative response while working on yourself?

3. Who in your life can support you and hold you accountable during this season? What makes this person a safe person?

4. What are five things you can apologize for? Don't forget to use the four-step apology structure we discussed as part of habit 8.

5. How has holding on to the pain and hurt your spouse
    has caused you impacted your life (mentally, emotion-
    ally, physically, spiritually)?

6. How do you want to show up in this marriage re-
    gardless of what your spouse chooses?

. . . Make a Better You

About five years into our marriage, we found ourselves broke, unemployed, and nearly homeless. We decided to move in with Meygan's mom. Not ideal for two adults who were supposed to be living their own lives with a nine-month-old child. It was embarrassing, discouraging, and scary. We had no idea how we were going to get through it. In so many ways, it should have been the lowest of the lows. But, surprisingly, it wasn't. We'd already done so much work to repair our marriage. And it paid off.

I (Casey) remember sitting outside on a perfectly warm summer day, watching my daughter and wife splash in that tiny kiddie pool we told you about earlier. The one we held to the top of our car with our arms out the windows. It was all we could afford that year, and it proved to be just what we needed. As I watched them, I looked at Meygan and thought how grateful I was to be with her and to have what we had. Years earlier, a thought like that would have been unimaginable.

As I pondered everything that was going "wrong" in our lives, I wasn't bitter or angry or resentful. I didn't blame her for our circumstances or wish that a million things had gone differently. Instead, I knew *I could never get through this without her.* I also knew we'd get through this season, not because we had a plan or any special skills to help us do so, but simply because we had each other—and the team we were together—and that was enough. Meygan glanced up at me, soaked from splashing, with her blond hair stuck to her face, and smiled. In what should have been the hardest season of my life, I had a refuge. And it wasn't a place. It was *her.* My person. My home. My wife.

This is what marriage feels like at its best. Over the course of your life, incredibly hard things will happen. You will lose jobs, people, opportunities, and maybe even your mind. You'll experience disappointments, rejection, and all kinds of letdowns. But when you have a healthy marriage, you have a shelter from the storm, a lighthouse in the fog, an anchor in the rough seas. No matter what, forever and ever, you have someone who is there for you, who cheers you on, and who catches you when you fall. You have a safe place to go.

That's a life-changing kind of love. In fact, it can even be generation changing. Imagine what would happen if every kid grew up in a home with that kind of relationship as a model. What if our kids watched us bless each other and forgive and have fun? I not-so-humbly submit that this would change the world. That's what's really at stake here.

Marriages create families that raise kids, who turn into adults and eventually run the world. If we want to raise a generation of adults who know how to love well, handle conflict, and build relationships that stand the test of time, it starts with us. It starts with you. It starts with the way we show up for our spouse, the way we communicate, the way we prioritize connection, even when life gets messy. Because the truth is, marriage isn't just about two people. It's about the legacy they create together. It's about the home they build—not just the four walls, but the way they define what love looks like, sounds like, and feels like.

When I sit across from a couple in crisis considering the future of their marriage, I remind them that the work they do today directly impacts three generations of their family. When a couple courageously choose to love each other, it impacts their kids, who grow up and find their own partners. And if those adult children choose to have kids, they will raise them with the confidence they inherited from their parents, and with the habits they grew up witnessing in mind.

So, as you take these ten habits and put them into practice, remember: This isn't just about having a better marriage (though that's a pretty great bonus). This is about changing the trajectory of your life. It's about small, intentional choices that add up to a whole new you.

We are so excited for your marriage to change and grow. Even more, we're excited to see how *you* change. You can be that shelter in the storm for each other. You can fall back in love and build something better than you ever imagined. One day, one decision, one habit at a time.

Life's too short to get this wrong. And there's too much at stake. Never forget: If you want to make a better marriage, make a better you.

ACKNOWLEDGMENTS

To Lucinda Halpern: Thank you for always believing in us and our vision to help couples build thriving, lasting marriages. Your steady support, wisdom, and belief in our message have meant the world to us. We're so grateful to have you by our side on this incredible journey. You've been more than a literary agent— you've been a true champion of our mission. This book wouldn't exist without you!

To Liz Morrow: You've been with us every step of the way— through the laughs, the disagreements, the rewrites, and the breakthroughs. You've seen it all, and somehow you still like us! This book wouldn't have happened—nor would it have made sense—without your talent, insight, and deep understanding of who we are and what we're about. You're more than a collaborator. You understand us so deeply, it's like you can read our minds. You often finish our sentences, and you've embraced who we are while helping bring our voice and ideas to life.

To our incredible staff at Marriage365: You've believed in us from the very beginning. You've prayed for us, listened to us, encouraged us, and stood by us through the highs, the lows, and all the emotional in-betweens. Your unwavering support reminds us that we can do hard things—and we don't have to do them alone. We're beyond blessed to walk this journey with people who love us deeply and share our vision for helping marriages thrive. Thank you for being our people.

To Derek: We might be biased, but we're convinced you're the best editor on the planet. You've challenged us to dig deeper, clarify our message, and say the hard things with heart. Your ability to refine our words while protecting our voice is a rare gift. And the fact that you take what you read and apply it to your own marriage? That means everything to us.

To the entire team at Convergent: Thank you for believing in us and our message. Your commitment to excellence and your genuine care made this process not only possible but deeply meaningful. We are honored to partner with you and so grateful for your role in helping us share hope, healing, and practical tools with couples everywhere.

To those who mentored us: Jim and Debbie Hogan, Rob and Rocki Maroney, Ron and Nan Deal, Travis and Carol Turner, Jim Burns, Drew Sherline, and Eric Heard. You believed in us when we didn't believe in ourselves. You've modeled what it means to have a healthy marriage, and you inspire us to fight the good fight. Thank you for imparting your life wisdom to us; it carries on through our mission.

NOTES

"WHY DOES THIS FEEL SO HARD?"

7 successful marriages aren't: Gary W. Lewandowski, Jr., "For Relationship Success, Argue More Not Less," *Psychology Today*, September 8, 2021, www.psychology today.com/us/blog/the-psychology-of-relationships/ 202109/for-relationship-success-argue-more-not -less.

8 aren't necessarily happier: Alois Stutzer and Bruno S. Frey, "Does Marriage Make People Happy, or Do Happy People Marry?" *The Journal of Socio-Economics* 35, no. 2 (2006): 326–47, https://doi.org/10.1016/j.socec.2005 .11.043.

9 "You never see": *Just Married*, directed by Shawn Levy (Twentieth Century Fox, 2003).

THE ONLY TWO THINGS YOU NEED

16   "Desire needs mystery": Esther Perel, *Mating in Captivity: Unlocking Erotic Intelligence* (HarperCollins, 2006), 36.

18   "the drift": Michael Hyatt, "How to Avoid the Power of the Drift," Full Focus, https://fullfocus.co/how-to-avoid -the-power-of-the-drift.

THE TEN HABITS

23   flywheel effect: This idea originated in Jim Collins's book *Good to Great: Why Some Companies Make the Leap . . . and Others Don't* (Harper Business, 2001).

24   "Baby steps": *What About Bob?*, directed by Frank Oz (Touchstone Pictures, 1991).

HABIT 1: THE KNOWN POSITION

26   55 percent of communication: Elizabeth Perry, "7-38-55 Rule of Communication: How to Use for Negotiation," BetterUp, May 15, 2023, www.betterup.com/blog/7-38-55 -rule; Albert Mehrabian, *Silent Messages* (1971; repr., Wadsworth Publishing Company, 1972).

26   "Sixty percent of all human": *Hitch*, directed by Andy Tennant, starring Will Smith (Columbia Pictures, 2005).

27   *The Artist Is Present*: Jim Dwyer, "Confronting a Stranger, for Art," *New York Times*, April 2, 2010, www.nytimes.com/ 2010/04/04/nyregion/04about.html.

27 the experience changed their lives: Tree Meinch, "We're Beginning to Understand the Power of Eye Contact," *Discover*, June 6, 2022, last updated March 17, 2023, www .discovermagazine.com/mind/were-beginning-to -understand-the-power-of-eye-contact.

30 "Never half-ass": *Parks and Recreation*, season 4, episode 16, "Sweet Sixteen," written by Greg Daniels et al., directed by Michael Schur, aired February 23, 2012, on NBC.

31 "kind of phase-locked": Meinch, "We're Beginning to Understand the Power of Eye Contact."

HABIT 2: THE WEEKLY MARRIAGE BUSINESS MEETING

37 less than thirty-five minutes: John M. Gottman and Nan Silver, *The Seven Principles for Making Marriage Work: A Practical Guide from the Country's Foremost Relationship Experts*, 2nd ed. (Harmony, 2015), 196. See also Kyle Benson, "4 Typical Solvable Relationship Problems," The Gottman Institute, April 7, 2017, last updated May 5, 2025, www.gottman.com/blog/4-typical-solvable -problems-relationships.

42 48 percent of couples: "Money, Marriage, and Communi- cation," Ramsey Solutions, September 27, 2021, www .ramseysolutions.com/relationships/money-marriage -communication-research.

45 save over $1,500: George Morris, "How to Make a Money Saving Meal Plan," last updated December 12, 2022,

InCharge Debt Solutions, www.incharge.org/financial
-literacy/budgeting-saving/money-saving-meal-plan.

47   no significant difference in satisfaction: Wendy Klein
     et al., "Working Relationships: Communicative Patterns
     and Strategies Among Couples in Everyday Life," *Qualita-
     tive Research in Psychology*, vol. 4, no. 1–2 (2007): 29–47,
     doi:10.1080/14780880701473391.

53   five types of love languages: Gary Chapman, *The 5 Love
     Languages* (Northfield Publishing, 1995).

HABIT 4: THE 60-SECOND BLESSING

68   "Death and life": Proverbs 18:21, Amplified Bible, by The
     Lockman Foundation, 2015.

68   five-to-one ratio: Kyle Benson, "The Magic Relationship
     Ratio, According to Science," The Gottman Institute,
     October 4, 2017, last updated September 18, 2024, www
     .gottman.com/blog/the-magic-relationship-ratio
     -according-science.

74   higher relationship satisfaction: A. M. Gordon et al., "To
     Have and to Hold: Gratitude Promotes Relationship
     Maintenance in Intimate Bonds," *Journal of Personality and
     Social Psychology* 103, no. 2 (2012), https://doi.org/10.1037/
     a0028723.

HABIT 5: CONNECTION TIME

82   joke about their sex lives: Christine D. Lomore et al.,
     "The Use of Sexual Humor in Romantic Relationships:

Description, Valence and Association with Sexual Satisfaction," *Canadian Journal of Human Sexuality* 33, no. 3 (2024), https://doi.org/10.3138/cjhs-2024-0024.

HABIT 6: LEVERAGE YOUR DIFFERENCES

93   hundreds of thousands of couples: Institute for Divorce Financial Analysts, "Survey: CDFA Professionals Reveal the Leading Causes of Divorce," *IDFA*, Aug 29, 2013, institutedfa.com/cdfa-professionals-reveal-leading-causes -of-divorce/.

HABIT 9: HEAD. HANDS. HEART. HABIT.

139 "I believe hate": "Mary Johnson and Oshea Israel," The Forgiveness Project, last updated April 11, 2024, www .theforgivenessproject.com/stories-library/mary-johnson -oshea-israel.

140 "Unforgiveness is like": Steve Hartman, "Love Thy Neighbor: Son's Killer Moves Next Door," CBS News, June 8, 2011, www.cbsnews.com/news/love-thy-neighbor -sons-killer-moves-next-door.

HABIT 10: THE SEX TALK

153 "Sex is an incredibly": Vanessa Marin, *Sex Talks: The Five Conversations That Will Transform Your Love Life* (Simon Element, 2023), 65.

ABOUT THE AUTHORS

CASEY AND MEYGAN CASTON are the husband-and-wife duo behind Marriage365, a movement that reaches millions of couples around the globe. Though they consider themselves an average married couple—with laundry piles, inside jokes, and their fair share of disagreements—they've spent the last thirteen years as certified life and marriage coaches studying success from some of the top relationship experts. They made it their mission to help others become the best version of themselves regardless of their circumstances. Their approach is honest, practical, and rooted in real-life experience. They don't just teach tools—they live them. Casey and Meygan believe that simple, clear steps can lead to real transformation.

They live in sunny Orange County, California, with their two kids. You'll often find them soaking up beach days or battling it out over a deck of cards.

ABOUT MARRIAGE365

We have a dream to see every couple who picks up this book become happy, connected, and understood by each other. It's what gets us up every morning! Our life's work is to help build healthy relationships and bring hope to those who desire to live to the fullest.

Just three years into marriage, we were voted the couple least likely to succeed. We literally hated each other! But we walked back from the brink of divorce. So take it from us: If we can build a healthy relationship centered around open-ended questions, you can too.

Our restored marriage inspired us to help other couples who were feeling stuck, lost, and confused about how to reconnect. Today, Marriage365 reaches millions of couples around the world, providing practical advice, resources, and inspiration. You can find all our resources by visiting marriage365.com.

Also available from

CASEY CASTON and MEYGAN CASTON

REVISED AND UPDATED

365

CONNECTING QUESTIONS FOR COUPLES

WITH 200 NEW QUESTIONS

CASEY & MEYGAN CASTON
Co-founders of MARRIAGE365

CONVERGENT